The Essential Horse Book

THE COMPLETE GUIDE

PHYSIOLOGY, WELL-BEING, CARE, DISEASE
AND
TACK FITMENT

LAURA A FITCH

First published in 2024 by Blue Horse Books, Union Dale, Pennsylvania

Copyright © 2024 Laura A. Fitch

All rights reserved. No portion of this book may be reproduced in any form without written permission from the publisher or author, except as permitted by U.S. copyright law.

Disclaimer of Liability

The author and publisher shall have neither liability nor responsibility to any person or entity with respect to loss or damage caused or alleged to be caused directly or indirectly by the information contained in this book. While the book is as accurate as the author can make it, there may be errors, omissions, and inaccuracies.

Library of congress Cataloging-In-Publication data

Name: Fitch, A. Laura, author

Title: The Essential Horse Book: The Complete Guide: A comprehensive resource for horse owners, trainers, and enthusiasts, covering key aspects of equine care, physiology, and management / Laura A Fitch with photographs and illustrations by Laura A Fitch except where noted.

Description: Union Dale, Pennsylvania: Blue Horse Books, 2024.| Summary: A renowned expert in equine bodywork, Laura A Fitch compiles her extensive knowledge and research from leading scientists and Universities into *The Essential Horse Book*. Dedicated to diet, housing, colic, laminitis, hoof care, saddle fitting, and more, this guide provides evidence-based practices and rich illustrations, making it and indispensable reference for maintaining a healthy and well-balanced horse.

Identifiers: LCCN 2024917896 | ISBN 9798991427104 (hardcover) | ISBN 9798991427111 (paperback) |

ISBN 9798991427128 (epub)

Photographs, Illustrations (except where noted), Book Design, and Cover Design by Laura A Fitch

Contents

Preface	IX
Dedication	XI
Part I	1
The Horse's Well-Being	
Introduction	3
Understanding the Horse: A Journey Back to Their Roots	
1. The Key to Equine Well-Being	5
Diet, Housing, Colic, Laminitis, and Founder	
Colic	
Causes of Colic	
Signs of Colic	
Laminitis and Founder	
Signs of Laminitis	
Diet and Management	
2. A Healthy Horse	17
Henneke Test, Temperature, Pulse, Respiration, Mucous Membranes and Capillary refill	
Average Vital Signs	
How To Take	
The Horse's Temperature	

How To Measure The Heart/Pulse Rate
How To Measure Respiration Rate/Breaths Per Minute

Mucous Membranes and Capillary Refill

PART II — 23
The Mind and Physiology of The Horse

3. The Equine Mind — 25
   How Horses Think, React, and Learn
   - How Horses Think
   - How Horses React
   - How Horses Learn
   - Perception of the Environment

4. Vision, Hearing, Smell — 33
   Monocular and Binocular Vision, Perception, Colors, Hearing, and Smell
   - Monocular and Binocular Vision
   - Perception
   - Colors
   - Hearing
   - Smell

5. Anatomy of The Horses's Teeth — 45
   Types of Teeth, Age of Tooth Eruption, Common Dental Issues
   - Types of Teeth
   - Estimating Age
   - The Most Common Dental Issues

6. The Digestive System — 59

The Horse's Stomach, Two Halves, Types of Ulcers, Signs of Ulcers, Starch In The Diet, Conclusion
   The Horse's Stomach
   ~ TWO HALVES ~
   Factors Affecting Digestive Health
   Signs of Ulcers
   Impact of Starch In The Diet
   Conclusion

7. The Equine Hoof   71
Balance, Wall, Bars, Frog, Lateral Cartilage, Digital Cushion, Angles, Heels, and Trimming
   Hoof Balance
   The Hoof Wall
   The Bars
   The Frog
   Lateral Cartilage
   Digital Cushion
   Medial/Lateral Balance
   Anterior/Posterior Balance
   Hoof Angle
   Heels
   Trimming to Internal Structures

8. A Guide To Parasite Prevention   83
Types of Worms, Parasite Management, How To Prevent Parasite Resistance
   Fecal Egg Count
   Types Of Worms
   Parasite Management

How To Prevent Parasite Resistance

9. The Best Sleep Practices — 89
   Two Stages of Sleep, Signs of Sleep Deprivation, Identifying The Root Cause
   - Two Stages Of Sleep
   - Signs Of Sleep Deprivation
   - Identifying The Root Cause
   - Resolution

Part III — 93
The Horse Owner's Guide To Tack Fitment

10. Bridle and Halter Fitting Guide — 95
    Cranial Nerves, Bridle and Halter Fitment, Facial and Ear Hair Rules
    - Facial Nerve Paralysis
    - Halter Fitting Guide
    - Facial Hair
    - Ear Hair

11. Saddle Fit — 107
    How-To-Guide, Skeletal Maturity, Saddle Fit for The Horse and Rider, Fitting a Breastplate, Measuring The Rider for Saddle Fit
    - Skeletal Maturity
    - Saddle Fit for The Horse and Rider
    - Measuring The Rider for Saddle Fit

12. English & Western Girth Fitment   119
    How-To-Guide
        How-To Measure For Girth Size
        Signs Your Girth May Not Fit

PART IV   127
The Horse's Coat

13. The Horse's Coat   129
    Heat and Humidity, Scratches, Rain Rot, Cooling, Hydration, Hay Consumption, and Blanketing
        Heat and Humidity
        Sweat
        Signs of Heat Exhaustion
        Signs Of Heat Stroke
        How-To Cool The Horse Down
        Wet Weather: Rain Rot And Scratches

About the author   147

Endnotes   148

PREFACE

The journey of understanding and caring for horses is both a rewarding and intricate endeavor. Over the years, as an Equine Body Work practitioner, I have had the privilege of working closely with hundreds of horses. Through these experiences, I have observed a recurring theme: horse owners, riders, and caregivers often struggle to find reliable, scientifically-backed information about their equine companions. They rely on guesswork, hearsay, and occasionally misguided advice, leading to challenges such as ulcers, sore backs, and other painful conditions for their horses.

The Essential Horse Book: The Complete Guide is born from the desire to bridge this knowledge gap. This book is crafted to serve as a comprehensive and dependable resource, offering well-documented scientific research from reputable veterinarians and universities. My aim is to provide accurate, trustworthy information that empowers horse owners to make informed decisions, enhancing the health and well-being of their beloved animals.

Designed with the reader in mind, this book features an array of charts, diagrams, and photos making it exceptionally user-friendly. The visuals not only simplify complex information but also allow readers to easily locate the help they need. Additionally, the utility of this book is amplified by its portability; not only in its handy size, but readers can take photos of the pertinent information with their phones, providing a quick reference whenever they are away from home.

I hope *The Essential Horse Book: The Complete Guide* becomes a valuable tool in your equine care arsenal, guiding you towards a deeper understanding and a more fulfilling relationship with your horse.

For the horse.
May we stop their needless suffering.
Allow them to graze freely under the sun, the moon, and the stars,
and roam the land with their relatives as a herd.
May they be treated with a gentle hand, and loving heart.
May we see them as the sentient beings that they are.
May they run free...

Part I
The Horse's Well-Being

Feral Nokota® horses on the plains of North Dakota

Introduction
Understanding the Horse: A Journey Back to Their Roots

You've been there, late at night in the stable feeling the gnawing worry that something isn't right with your horse. You've seen them shift uncomfortably, their usually bright eyes clouded with unease. You know the frustration of pouring your heart into their care, only to be met with unexplained health issues that leave you questioning everything you thought you knew.

But imagine a different scenario. Your horse, vibrant and healthy moving with a grace that turns heads. You no longer worry about the small signs because you've learned to read them, and to understand your horse on a level few achieve. You feel a deep satisfaction knowing that your horse isn't just surviving but thriving. The time you spend together is full of joy, free from the constant shadow of what-if.

In *The Essential Horse Book: The Complete Guide* you'll gain the knowledge to make this your reality. You'll learn how to recognize the early signs of common but serious issues like colic and laminitis. How to ensure your horse's diet supports optimal health, and how proper fitment of tack can prevent long-term physical problems. This book is a roadmap to transforming your horse's care. From the basics of daily maintenance to the complexities of equine health that often go unnoticed.

My journey into writing this book started with a simple, yet profound realization: horses are incredibly resilient, but also incredibly vulnerable. With years of experience and multiple certifications in equine bodywork and care. I've spent my life learning how to unlock the secrets to keeping horses not just alive, but flourishing. This book is the culmination of that journey-a guide meant to equip you with the tools and knowledge to provide the best possible care for your horse.

Now, it's your turn. As you delve into the pages of *The Essential Horse Book: The Complete Guide* you'll be taking the first step towards becoming the kind of caretaker who can anticipate your horse's needs, solve problems before they start, and build a relationship that is both rewarding and fulfilling. Let's embark on this journey together, because you and your horse deserve nothing less.

Feral Nokota® horses on the plains of North Dakota

I

The Key to Equine Well-Being

Diet, Housing, Colic, Laminitis, and Founder

Imagine standing at the edge of a vast, untamed meadow at dawn, where the horizon stretches into infinity. Wild horses have thrived here for centuries, living not by constraints of fences but by the natural laws of the land. These magnificent creatures move as one, a seamless blend of power and grace. Navigating the perils and pleasures of the range with an unspoken unity that only a life lived together as a herd can bring. In *The Essential Horse Book*, we delve deep into the essence of what makes these horses not just survivors, but symbols of the freedom and harmony that many seek to recreate in the domesticated world. Understanding this natural life is the cornerstone of good horse management.

Just as humans thrive on physical activity, a healthy diet, and proper sleep, horses have their own needs that are deeply rooted in their nature. As herd animals, they are inherently social and dependent on their group for companionship and safety. In the wild, they would never live alone or be confined; instead, they exist in tightly knit herds, grazing, playing, and socializing. This is the true essence of a horse's life, and by embracing this understanding, we can foster their well-being in our care.

A typical herd consists of 3 to 10 horses, including a dominant stallion, other adult males, mares, and their foals. This close-knit family unit moves as one, grazing, visiting watering holes, playing, grooming, and protecting each other from danger. These natural behaviors-grazing, resting, and grooming-are essential to their well-being.[1]

In contrast, domesticated horses often face a starkly different reality. While their wild counterparts might spend up to 19 hours a day foraging and can travel an average of 15 miles per day, domesticated horses frequently have their natural behaviors curtailed with restricted movement, limited forage, and isolation due to seperation and/or stalling.

Researchers have found that domesticated horses allowed to graze freely spend more than half their day foraging and engaging in other natural behaviors, such as socializing, grooming, and playing with other herd members. This freedom is crucial for their physical and mental health. However, when foraging is restricted, such as a study done with small box feeders that make hay access difficult, horses became aggressive, leading to abnormal behaviors. These behaviors include, cribbing, stall walking, kicking stall walls, chewing, licking, and even shutting down mentally—actions rarely seen in wild horses.[2]

Preventing stereotypical behaviors in horses largely depends on proper housing and management. Like their wild counterparts, domesticated horses thrive when they have regular contact with others for mutual grooming and the opportunity to graze freely in a paddock or pasture with access to forage, without the inclusion of grains or concentrates. This natural lifestyle helps to prevent the developement of abnormal behaviors.[3]

Housing conditions significantly influence a horse's behavior and learning abilities. When deprived of social interaction and confined to a stall, a horse can develop stereotypic behaviors such as cribbing, weaving and stall walking. Studies have shown that young horses kept on pasture are easier to train, require less riding time, are more responsive, and buck less than those kept in stalls. Moreover, stalling horses has been shown to negatively impact bone formation, regardless of age.[4]

Additionally, horses with large pasture turnout travel greater distances and maintain their body weight and condition better than those confined to stalls, who often lose fitness despite forced weekly excercise.[5] By understanding and accomodating these natural behaviors, we can ensure the well-being and happiness of the horses in our care.

> Restricted movement, grain-based feeding, and social isolation can lead to chronic stress states, causing behavioral problems, physical and metabolic disorders, and changes in immune response in horses. Insufficient forage amounts can also lead to abnormal behaviors like wood chewing, along with alterations in immune cell numbers and cortisol levels.[6]

Horses naturally crave social interaction and prefer living in groups. When they are allowed to roam freely in pastures and graze with other horses, they benefit from a structured social environment. A 1000-pound horse typically needs 2 to 4 acres of pasture to meet its foraging needs.[7] If pasture space is limited, solutions like Track Systems that mimic the lifestyle of a free, wild-roaming horse can provide horses with areas to excercise and live together, encouraging movement as they seek out hay at hay stations, water, rolling areas, and shelter.[8]

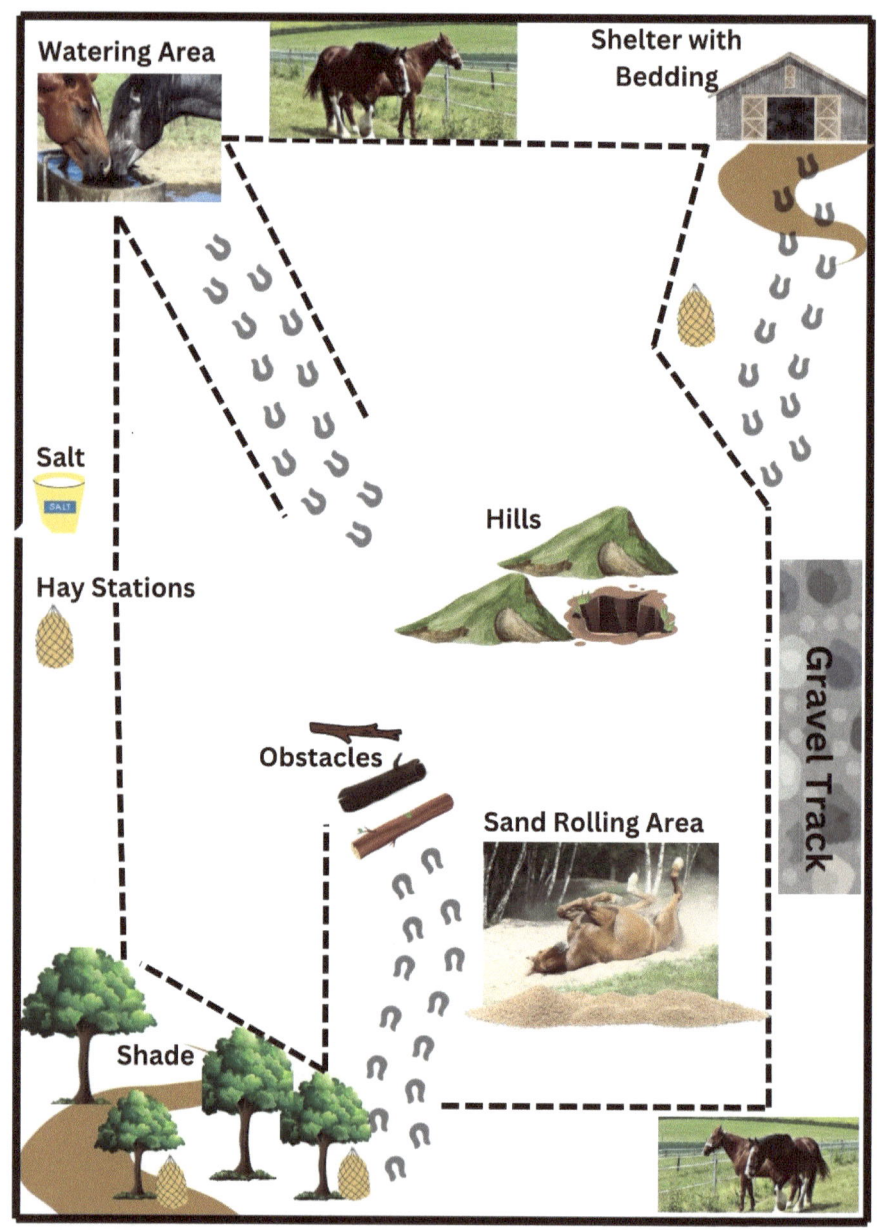

Track System

THE KEY TO EQUINE WELL-BEING

Other solutions to prevent stalling that promote socialization and movement include attaching fence lines to the barn or shelter, while leaving the barn and stall doors open to allow free roaming with access to pasture, water, and other horses, ensuring a structured social environment.

Modern management practices often confine horses to stalls, limiting their exercise and feeding them grain-based diets instead of forage-based ones. These changes in diet and confinement have resulted in various health issues, such as bone loss, abnormal behaviors, and diseases like ulcers, laminitis, founder and colic.[9]

> Horses are naturally designed to eat a diet rich in fiber from forages, which provide most of their energy. High-starch diets can disrupt the gut's natural balance, causing conditions like, colic, gastric ulcers, and even severe muscle disorders, additionally researchers link high cereal grain intake to oxidative stress, which is a marker of poor animal welfare.[10]

COLIC

Colic is one of the leading causes of death in horses, described as any type of abdominal pain in the horse.

There are 3 types of colic:

1. Gas Colic: caused by gas build-up in the large colon and cecum.

2. Spasmodic Colic: caused by spasms in the intestinal walls.

3. Impaction Colic: caused by a blockage in the intestine from digested feed, and often due to poor quality hay, sand, or dental issues from improper chewing.

Twisted Intestine occurs when the horse's colon or intestine is twisted or strangulated, requiring surgical intervention.

Colic can also result from inflammation of the small intestine or colon, colitis, diarrhea, and gastric ulcers. Gastric ulcers can cause intermittent mild colic episodes, with signs such as colic after eating grain, poor performance, and a dull coat. Preventing gastric ulcers includes maximizing turnout and providing access to pasture or hay 24/7, while avoiding grain.

CAUSES OF COLIC

- Intestinal Parasites: A high number of *Roundworms* can cause impaction.

- Tapeworms: can obstruct the passage of food.

- Sudden Diet Changes.

- Feeding Grain: Increases gut fermentation and causes gas build-up.

- Inadequate forage and fiber intake.

- Late-harvested hay harvested with too many stalks and insufficient leaves can cause impaction.

- Dehydration due to insufficient water intake can cause impaction.

- Horses kept in stalls are at a higher risk for colic.[11]

SIGNS OF COLIC

- Biting or kicking at the sides or belly.
- Pawing.
- Lying down or rolling excessively.
- Looking at the sides.
- Refusal to eat or drink.
- Little or no passing of manure.
- Passing dry or mucous-covered manure.
- Heart rate over 45- 50 beats per minute.
- Tacky gums.
- Prolonged capillary refill time of the gums.
- Off-colored mucous membranes.[12]

At signs of colic:

- This is a medical emergency: Call your veterinarian.

- Remove the horse's feed and allow access to water. Check the horse's respiration, heart rate, and temperature.

- Examine the horse's gums for color; healthy gums are pink and moist.

- Walk the horse to prevent injury from rolling in a stall.

Another common ailment in horses is Laminitis and Founder.

LAMINITIS AND FOUNDER

Laminitis is extremely painful condition and constitutes a medical emergency. Call a veterinarian immediately.

Laminitis is the sudden onset of pain and inflammation in the laminar structures in the hoof. Founder occurs when laminitis is prolonged, causing the coffin bone to rotate or to sink towards the sole of the hoof.

Horses consuming excessive grain or processed feeds, like pelleted grains, lush pastures, or hay with high sugar content are highly suseptable to laminitis and founder. The horse's *foregut (*small intestine*)*, may struggle to process the large influx of carbohydrates, leading to undigested starch and sugars passing rapidly into the hindgut. This imbalance disrupts the digestive microbiome, potentially resulting in *colic, laminitis, or both.* Other causes include contact with black walnut shavings, excessive impact on hard surfaces, obesity, stress, and overconsumption of cold water by overheated horses.[13]

Types of laminitis:

1. Endocrinopathic (hyperinsulinemia-associated): Excessive insulin affects the hoof's laminar epideral cell structure.

2. Sepsis-related laminitis: Acute diseases like colitis, pneumonia, or metritis, particularly with an inflammatory component (endotoxemia).

3. Supporting-limb laminitis: Limb fractures altering weight-bearing patterns affecting limb.[14]

SIGNS OF LAMINITIS

Signs of laminitis include:
- Reluctance to move, or stand.
- Frequent lying down.
- Stands with front legs stretched out in front and, or behind.
- Shifting weight from one hoof to another frequently.
- Increased breathing and heart rate.
- Heat in the hooves.
- Increased digital pulse.

Stages of laminitis:

There are typically three stages of laminitis:
- Developmental Stage: Initial injury to the laminae, which may go unnoticed.

- Acute Stage: Signs of lameness appear, possibly accompanied by coffin bone rotation, increased breathing and heart rate, elevated digital pulse, heat in the hooves and limb swelling.

- Chronic Stages: Symptoms persist for over a week, with pain and lameness caused by coffin bone displacement. Hoof changes may include a dished appearance, growth rings, white line separation, seedy toe, and abscesses. In severe cases, the coffin bone may penetrate through the sole of the hoof.

Treatment of Pain:

- Pain management may involve non-steroidal anti-inflammatory drugs, opiates, ice baths, or ice boots to reduce inflammation and pain.

- Soaking hay in lukewarm water for 60 minutes, draining, rinsing and air-drying before feeding reduces soluble sugar content by 30-35%.

- Confining horses to dry lots with soft bedding until their condition improves is also recommended.

- Do not feed any grains, supplements, or cool-season legume grasses such as, rye, alfalfa and clover.

- Proper hoof care is crucial in the recovery of laminitis.

DIET AND MANAGEMENT

- Feed hay and pasture with a low non-structural carbohydrate content.

- Avoid feeding grain.

- Regular hoof care (approximately every 4 weeks).

- Manage weight to prevent obesity.[15]

Plant sugars are highest in the late afternoon and lowest in the early morning. For horses suseptable to laminitis, grazing times are best between 3 am and 10 am. Most pasture grasses store sugars in the bottom 3-4 inches of growth; short grasses and weeds are directly linked to laminitis due to high sugar content. Grasses most likely to accumulate sugars are timothy, bromegrass, orchardgrass, and many cool-season grasses like alfalfa, clover, and rye grass. Research at Western Kentucky University found that horses consuming ryegrass gained weigth, had increased body condition scores, and elevated insulin secretion.[16] Sugar content (carbohydrates) peaks in immature grasses in early spring, during regrowth, cool nights with warm sunny days, and after a hard freeze or during drought conditions.[17]

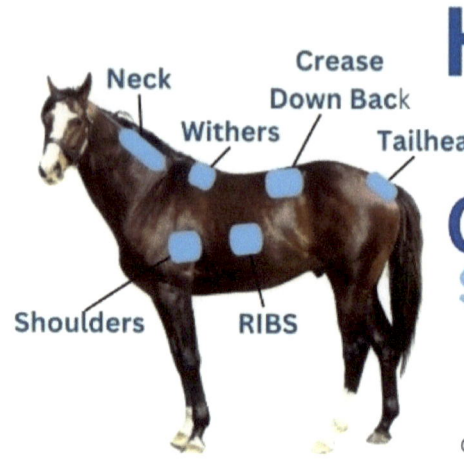

HENNEKE BODY CONDITION SCORING SYSTEM

The scoring system is used by law enforcement agencies and veterinarians as an objective method of scoring a horse's body condition in horse cruelty cases.

SCORE	Description
1-3	Poor health, skinny and malnourished.
4	Ribs visible with the vertebrae ridge showing.
5	Ribs can be felt but not seen, with fat deposits and a crease down the back.
6	Normal healthy horse with moderate fat and not too thin.
7-9	Extremely fat horse with fatty deposits behind the shoulders, along the neck, withers, top of the tail, and flank, which can lead to metabolic issues like laminitis.

2

A Healthy Horse

Henneke Test, Temperature, Pulse, Respiration, Mucous Membranes and Capillary refill

Some signs of a healthy horse include its coat, which should be shiny and soft to the touch, its hooves should be without lines or chips and trimmed on a regular schedule, approximately every four weeks. The horses eyes should be bright and clear, and its ears upright and forward. The horse should also be adequately drinking 10 or more gallons of water a day, have access to forage 24/7 and its gums pink and moist. Additionally, it should have firm manure balls and maintain a healthy weight, scoring a 6 on the Henneke Horse Body Condition Score. Scores range from 1 (poor) to 9 (extremely fat). The scoring system is used by law enforcement agencies and veterinarians as an objective method of scoring a horse's body condition in horse cruelty cases.[1]

The Henneke Test assesses body fat on a scale from 1-9:

- 1-3: Poor health, skinny and malnourished.
- 4 : Ribs visible with the vertebrae ridge showing.
- 5: Ribs can be felt but not seen, with fat deposits and a crease down the back.

- 6: Normal healthy horse with moderate fat and not too thin.

- 7-9: Extremely fat horse with fatty deposits behind the shoulders, along the neck, withers, top of the tail, and flank, which can lead to metabolic issues like laminitis.[2]

AVERAGE VITAL SIGNS

ADULT HORSE:
- Temperature: 99-101.5°F
- Heart/Pulse: 28-44 beats per minute
- Respiration/Breaths: 10-24 breaths per minute

FOAL:
1. Temperature: 99.0-102.0°F
2. Heart/Pulse: 70-110 beats per minute
3. Respiration/Breaths: 30-40 beats per minute

HOW TO TAKE THE HORSE'S TEMPERATURE

The horse's temperature is taken rectally with a digital or mercury thermometer. First, cover the thermometer with lube, and insert the thermometer rectally. Wait until the thermometer reading is complete per instructions. It should be between 99-101.5 degrees Fahrenheit in an adult horse.

HORSE VITALS

TEMPERATURE
A normal adult horse at rest
99-101.5
Degrees Fahrenheit

Pulse
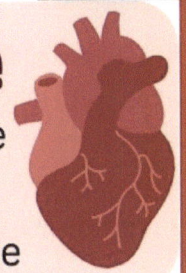
Adult Horse
35-40
Beats/Minute

Respiration

10-24 Adult Horse
Breaths/Minute

Skin Pliability
1-3
Seconds for skin to return

Mucous Membranes
Wet, Pink, Shiny Gums

Capillary Refill

1-2
Seconds
For color to return

by Laura A Fitch

How to Measure the Heart/Pulse Rate

Measure the horse's heart beat by using a stethoscope or by feeling the horse's artery if a stethoscope is not available. Put the stethoscope ear pieces in your ears, and then place the chest piece behind the horse's elbow on its left side until you hear its heart beating. Then count how many times you hear a beat (lub-dub sound) for thirty seconds. Each lub-dub counts as one beat. Then, multiply the number of beats by two and this will be how many beats per minute.

To check the horse's heart rate by an artery, there are three arteries; under the jaw bone (the maxillary artery), inside the knee (radial artery), and just below the fetlock (digital artery). Place your ring, middle or index finger on one of the arteries to feel the pulse of blood flow. Count each pulse for thirty seconds and multiply that number by two to determine how many beats per minute. If the horse is having trouble standing still, you can count the pulse beats for fifteen seconds and multiply that number by four to get the beats per minute. It should be between 28-44 beats per minute in an adult horse.

How to Measure Respiration Rate/Breaths Per Minute

The horse's respiration rate is measured in how many breaths the horse takes in one minute. Look at the horse's flank and count how many breaths the horse takes in and out in thirty-seconds. Multiply this number by two, and this will give you how many breaths per minute. It should be between 10-24 breaths per minute in an adult horse.[3]

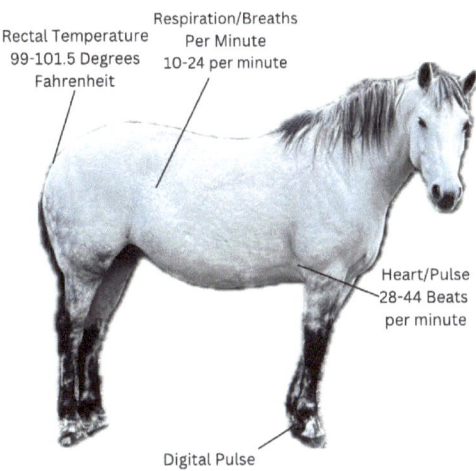

Counting the breaths of the horse at the flank is much more accurate than counting the horses breaths at the nostrils.

MUCOUS MEMBRANES AND CAPILLARY REFILL

The mucous membranes are evaluated to determine the hydration levels in the horse by checking at the gums in the mouth for color, texture, and wetness. In a healthy well-hydrated horse, the gums will be shiny, wet and pink. Dehydration is indicated by dry, pale and tacky gums, requiring veterinary consultation.

Capillary refill of the gums should take 1-2 seconds. This measures how quickly blood flow returns to the tissue after the gums are pressed and released. If it takes longer than 3 seconds, veterinarian advice should be sought.[4]

PART II

THE MIND AND PHYSIOLOGY OF THE HORSE

3

THE EQUINE MIND
HOW HORSES THINK, REACT, AND LEARN

HOW HORSES THINK

Horses possess a range of cognitive abilities that enable them to solve problems, remember past experiences, and navigate their environment. Research has shown that horses can engage in associative learning, where they form connections between stimuli and responses.[1] They also demonstrate the ability to understand concepts such as "same" and "different" in certain contexts, indicating a level of abstract thinking.[2]

As herd animals, horses are highly attuned to social cues and relationships. They can recognize individual herd members and form complex social bonds. Horses also exhibit social learning, where they learn behaviors by observing others, particularly when it comes to feeding or avoiding danger.[3]

The limbic system, particularly the amygdala, plays a central role in processing emotions influencing equine behavior, driving their flight response when faced with potential threats. Horses also experience other emotions such as anxiety, excitement, and even a form of empathy, where they can sense the emotions of other horses or humans.[4]

How Horses React

The Flight Response:

The flight response is the primary survival mechanism in horses, triggered by the sympathetic nervous system during perceived danger. When a horse perceives a threat, the amygdala signals the hypothalamus to initiate a cascade of physiological changes, including increased heart rate, adrenaline release, and muscle readiness, preparing the horse to flee.[5] This reaction is almost instantaneous and can be challenging to manage during training or handling.

Startle Reflex and Habituation:

The startle reflex is another survival mechanism, where sudden, unexpected stimuli cause an involuntary reaction, such as jumping or bolting. However, horses can become habituated to stimuli that are repeatedly presented without negative consequences, reducing their reactivity over time.[6] Habituation is a key concept in training, as it allows horses to learn that certain stimuli are not threatening.

Coping with Stress:

Horses cope with stress in various ways, depending on their environment, training, and past experiences. Chronic stress can lead to behavioral issues such as cribbing, weaving, or aggression. It's essential to provide horses with a stable, predictable environment and to use training methods that minimize stress to promote their well-being.[7]

How Horses Learn

Classical and Operant Conditioning:
Horses learn through both classical and operant conditioning. In classical conditioning, an animal learns to associate a neutral stimulus with a significant one, such as associating the sound of a bell with feeding time (Pavlovian response). Operant conditioning, on the other hand, involves learning through the consequences of behavior, such as receiving a reward for performing a desired reaction.[8] These principles are foundational in equine training.

Positive and Negative Reinforcement:
Reinforcement is a crucial aspect of learning in horses. Positive reinforcement involves rewarding a horse for a desired behavior, increasing the likelihood of the behavior being repeated. Negative reinforcement involves the removal of an aversive stimulus when the desired behavior is performed. Also, increasing the likelihood of the behavior being repeated.[9] For example, releasing pressure on the reins when a horse responds correctly is a form of negative reinforcement.

Timing and Consistency:
Timing and consistency are critical factors in equine learning. Horses are most likely to associate their behavior with a consequence if the reinforcement occurs immediately after the behavior. Consistent application of reinforcement helps the horse to understand what is expected of them, reducing confusion and frustration.[10]

Sympathetic and Parasympathetic Systems:

The horses ability to learn and form meaningful associations is deeply tied to their nervous system states, specifically the balance between sympathetic ("fight or flight") and parasympathetic ("rest and digest") systems. When a horse experiences stress, it activates the sympathetic nervous system, increasing heart rate and releasing adrenaline. However, effective training hinges on helping the horse return to a parasympathetic state, which fosters relaxation, reflection, and learning.

Research highlights that dopamine plays a key role in rewarding behaviors during learning. For example, when a horse successfully completes a task, dopamine is released, creating a "feel good" response. This encourages the horse to associate the task with a positive outcome, reinforcing the learning experience. At the same time, serotonin helps balance the horse emotionally, supporting the shift from arousal back to a calm state. This transition to a parasympathetic state is crucial for considering new knowledge. Leaving the horse relaxed after training allows it to process what it has learned more effectively, forming deeper associations for future recall.

Studies also emphasize the importance of creating coherence between the horse's emotional and physiological states. Practices like deep breathing, rhythmic activities, or even grooming sessions help synchronize the horse's nervous system, promoting relaxation and supporting better cognitive function. The "flow state" makes the learning experience smoother and more rewarding, aligning physiological balance with mental engagement.

Incorporating these insights into training sessions, by rewarding positive behaviors and ensuring the horse time for rest, creates optimal conditions for learning. This approach leverages the power of dopamine and serotonin while avoiding prolonged activation of the sympathetic ("fight or flight") system, which could lead to stress and hinder learning outcomes.

Horses take time to process information before responding to a stimulus. For example, research suggests that horses are more likely to learn through observation, but they do so at their own pace, processing the information they gather from their enviornment or other horses. Furthermore sensory and motor laterality, reveals that horses may use different sides of their brain to process various types of information. For instance, they tend to rely on their more reactive right brain hemisphere for emotional responses and their left hemisphere for more rational, calculated decisions. This lateralization might explain why horses seem to need more time in certain learning situations, as they process the information differently depending on context and stress levels. [11], [12]

> Thus, longer rest periods between decisions appear to promote deeper learning by giving the brain more time to process and integrate information from previous outcomes. [13]

Cognitive Bias and Problem-Solving:
Recent studies have shown that horses are capable of cognitive bias, where their emotional state influences how they interpret ambiguous stimuli. Horses in positive environments may perceive uncertain situations more optimistically, while those in stressful conditions may respond more negatively.[14] This understanding is crucial for training, as it emphasizes the importance of maintaining a positive, stress-free environment.

Horses also demonstrate problem-solving abilities, particularly in tasks that involve learning from previous experiences. For instance, horses can learn to navigate a maze to reach s food reward, adjusting their behavior based on trial and error.[15] This indicates a level of cognitive flexibility and memory retention.

The Importance of Patience and Understanding:
Training a horse requires patience and a deep understanding of equine cognition and emotions. Recognizing that a horse may react based on instinctual fears or past experiences can help trainers approach challenges with empathy. Building trust through positive experiences and gradual exposure to new stimuli can enhance learning and strengthen the bond between horse and handler.[16]

PERCEPTION OF THE ENVIRONMENT

The Importance of Contextual Cues:
Horses are highly sensitive to contextual cues in their environment. They use these cues to anticipate what might happen next, which is why they are often described as "creatures of habit." Horses can quickly learn routines and become stressed if their environment changes unpredictably.[17]

Emotional Perception and Communication:
Horses communicate their emotional states through body language, vocalization, and pheromones. They can also perceive the emotional states of other horses and even humans. For example, horses are known to mirror the emotional tone of their handlers, becoming more relaxed and anxious depending on the handler's demeanor.[18]

Stress and Learning:
Stress significantly impact a horse's ability to learn. Acute stress, such as that caused by a sudden threat, triggers the flight response,

which can override learned behaviors. Chronic stress, on the other hand, can lead to learned helplessness, where the horse becomes apathetic and unresponsive to training.[19]

Spatial Memory and Navigation:
The hippocampus in the horse's brain plays an integral role in spatial memory and navigation, especially due to the horse's reliance on spatial cues in pasture environments or while navigating trails. Horses create a mental map of their surroundings and use landmarks for orientation. The hippocampus is critical in forming and retaining long-term memories associated with both positive and negative experiences. Horses can remember stressful situations, such as those involving fear, confinement, or physical discomfort, which can lead to prolonged stress responses even after the initial experience has ended. They can also recall people, locations and specific stimuli associated with such events.[20, 21] Horses possess a highly detailed memory, particularly for negative experiences. They can recall specific sensory cues, such as the smell of a veterinarian or the sound of a farrier's truck. This precise recall helps them to anticipate and prepare for situations that may be uncomfortable, demonstrating how detail oriented their hippocampal memory can be.[22]

The equine mind is complex, shaped by millions of years of evolution as a prey species. Understanding how horses think, react, and learn allows us to approach their care and training with greater empathy and effectiveness. By acknowledging their cognitive abilities, emotional processing, and unique learning mechanisms, we can foster a more harmonious and mutually beneficial relationship with these remarkable animals.

4

VISION, HEARING, SMELL

MONOCULAR AND BINOCULAR VISION, PERCEPTION, COLORS, HEARING, AND SMELL

Did you know horses can only see TWO COLORS?

Horses can see *blue, green* and variations of these colors, but they cannot see the color *red* or any shades of red.

They possess about 50% better *night vision* than humans. When light enters their eyes, it triggers a photoreceptor on their retina called the *tapetum lucidum*, which enhances light sensitivity in low-light conditions. Their pupils become smaller or constrict in bright sunlight, reducing resolution and causing blurred vision, which makes it challenging for them to adjust their eyes when moving from light to dark environments.[1] This sensitivity may explain why horses can be reluctant to enter darker spaces like indoor arenas, stalls, or trailers.

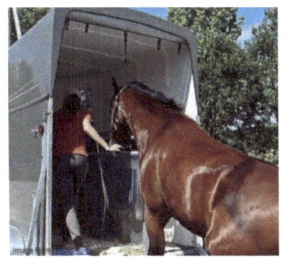

The horse transitioning from bright outdoor light to the inside of a dark trailer.

MONOCULAR AND BINOCULAR VISION

Horses have two types of vision: *Monocular* and *Binocular.* As prey animals, horses need to detect threats quickly and escape danger. Their large eyes are some of the largest eyes of all land mammals, approximately two inches in diameter, set wide apart and can move independently, providing *monocular vision* (seeing with one eye) that covers a wide arc of approximately 200-210 degrees around their body. This wide field of view helps detect motion from all sides, triggering their flight response if they perceive danger. However, they have two blind spots-one directly in front of them and another directly behind.

The area directly in front of the horse, from eye level to the ground and extending about 6-12 inches forward, is particularly blind to them. Quick movements in these blind spots can startle a horse, causing them to flinch or throw their head. Similarly, sudden movements directly behind a horse can cause them to spook, flee, or kick out for protection. For safety, it's important never to approach or stand directly behind a horse.

Binocular vision (seeing with two eyes at the same time) in horses is required to see depth perception and overlaps slightly in front of their face, but it doesn't provide accurate depth perception. Horses adjust their head position-raising it to see into the distance and lowering it to focus on objects close to the ground to enhance their range of vision and depth perception. They can see objects clearly up to about 20 feet away, whereas humans with normal vision can see clearly up to 30-60 feet.

PERCEPTION

Horses have two blind spots; one directly in front of them, and one directly behind them. The blind spot in front of the horse is from eye level to the ground

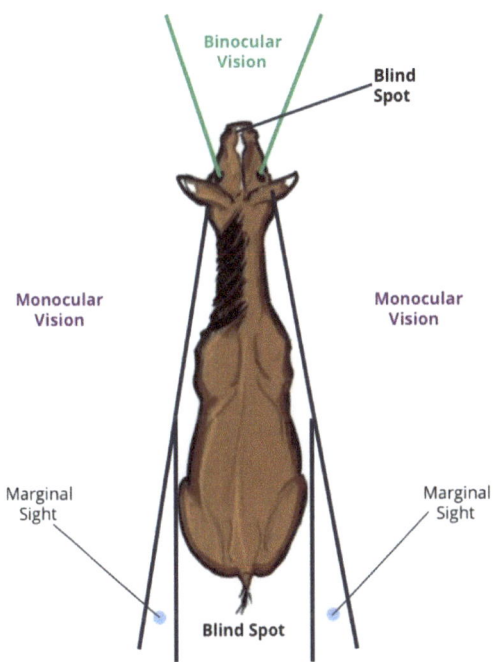

below their nose and out in front of their body about 6-12 inches. The horse cannot see the ground below his nose when grazing or things placed in front of his face. Quick movements in front of the horse's face may cause them to flinch or throw their head.

Quick or unknown movements directly behind the horse may startle them causing them to spook, runaway, or kick out behind themselves for protection. This is why we should never approach or stand directly behind a horse.

One study concluded that horses may react more strongly to new orientations of familiar objects, potentially leading to accidents and injuries for both the horse and handler. By preparing handlers and riders to anticipate these reactions, training methods can be adjusted to allow horses to investigate objects from all angles, reducing risks. Although horses show decreased reactions over time to novel objects and new orientations of familiar objects, reactions can still occur during the habituation process. Further research is recommended to explore how different handling and training techniques influence horses' responses to environmental changes. [2]

COLORS

Horses have limited color vision compared to humans. They can distinguish between blue and yellow hues but cannot perceive red, orange, or green colors unless they differ significantly in brightness. Research has shown that horses prefer blue-colored objects and lighter tones over darker ones. For example, they prefer drinking from blue-colored buckets over other colors, and light-toned colors over darker ones.

Providing a more pleasing water bucket color for your horse may encourage them to drink more.

Below is a graph of the horse's color preferences.

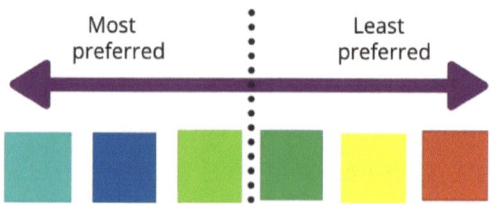

VISION, HEARING, SMELL

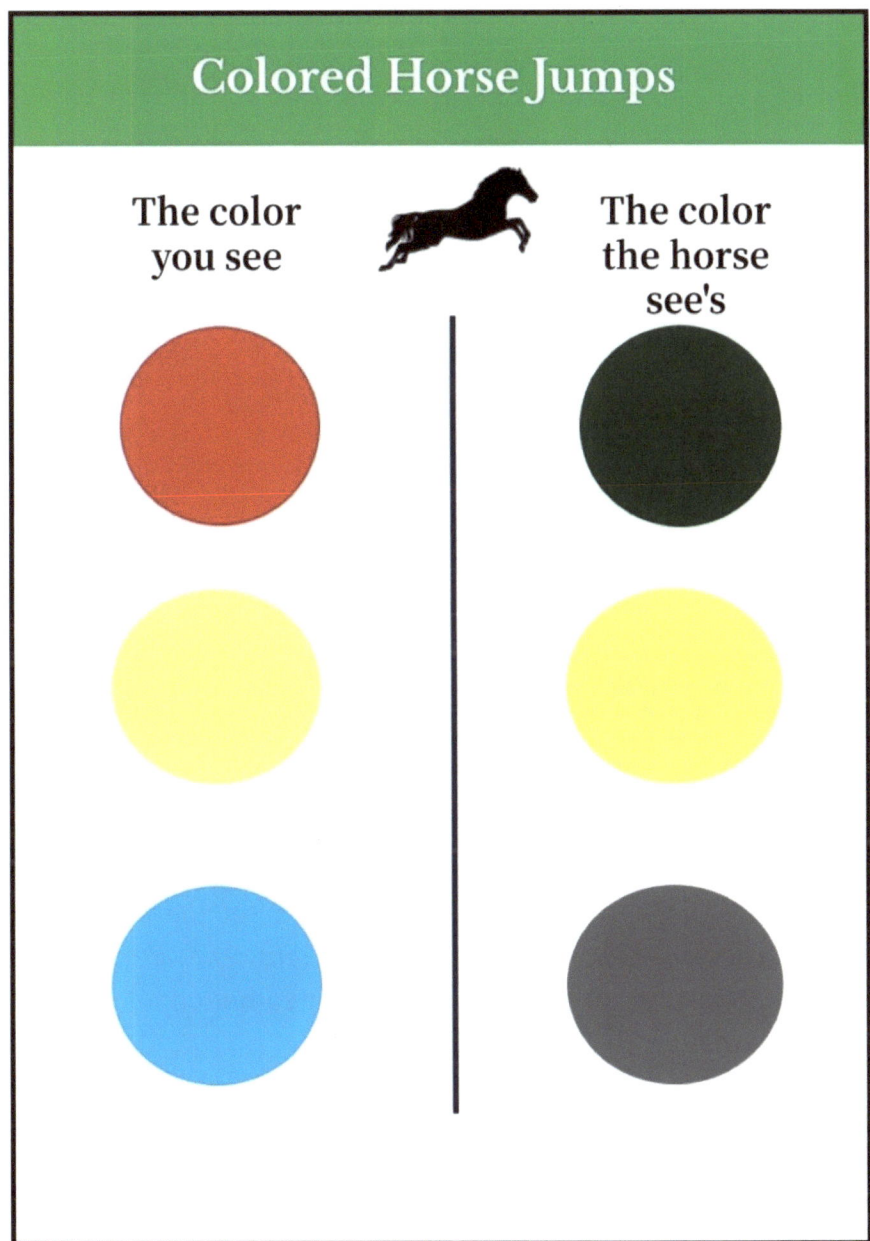

Horses have reduced color vision compared to humans, they can see a range of colors from blue to yellow, but they cannot distinguish between the colors red, orange, and green unless they differ in brightness.

The color of jumping fence poles significantly affects the way a horse jumps over them regarding take-off and landing distances, according to what researchers have reported in the journal, *Applied Animal Behavior Science*. They found that *fluorescent yellow* had the greatest contrast, maximizing the light and weather conditions, and making it easier for the horse to see.

Highly *illuminating whites or blues* at the base of a jump also provided *high contrast* making them more visible for the horse, and easier for the horse to take-off and land.[3]

DID YOU KNOW?
Horses Can't See RED

Human Trichromatic Color Vision

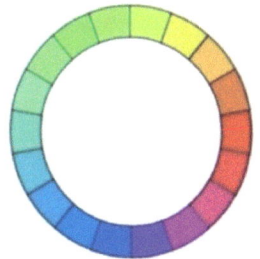

Horse Dichromatic Color Vision

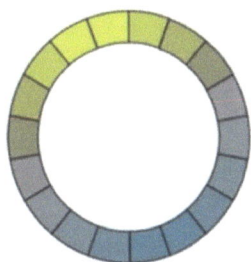

The left color wheel represents the spectrum of colors perceived by the trichromatic human visual system (three cones)

The wheel on the right, reducing the number of types of cones from three to two, results in dichromatic color vision, and a reduction in the number of different colors that can be seen by the horse.

Hearing

A horse's hearing is similar to humans but more sensitive to lower and higher-frequency sounds, with a range of *14 HZ to 25 kHz*. By rotaing their ears up to 180 degrees, horses can pinpoint the direction of sounds, aiding their ability to detect potential threats and flee from danger. Recent studies have discovered that horses can distinguish between different emotional tones in human voices, preferring calm, soothing tones over harsh ones. They also respond to human facial expressions and auditory cues, indicating recognition of familiar individuals based on vocal cues alone.

Studies suggest that older horses aged 15 to 18 years old had fewer behavior reactions to sounds than younger horses aged 5-9. They also found that as a horse's hearing impaired with age, prompting them to compensate by enhancing other senses, such as vision, for navigation and communication.

It is important to remember that a horse's hearing ability can weaken with age, and a horse trained with voice commands may have some difficulty following directions.[4, 5, 6, 7]

The flehmen response (curling the lip)

SMELL

Horses rely heavily on their sense of smell for survival and social interactions. Their olfactory system helps them detect safe food, avoid harmful substances, and recognize other horses by scent, including determining sex and reproductive status. Horses are nose breathers, and cannot breathe through their mouths. They have a large nasal cavity that contains a network of bony structures called turbinates, they are a network of bones, vessels, and tissue that help warm, humidify and cleanse the air they breath in, enhancing scent detection. With about 300 million olfactory receptors-much more than humans- horses process a broad range of scents. They also have an accessory vomeronasal organ that detects pheromones, triggering the flehmen response, where they curl their lip. This response helps horses further analyze strong odors, which can aid in identifying predators, estrous cycles, and familiar individuals, including people. Allowing a horse to sniff objects or people can ease their anxiety.[8],[9]

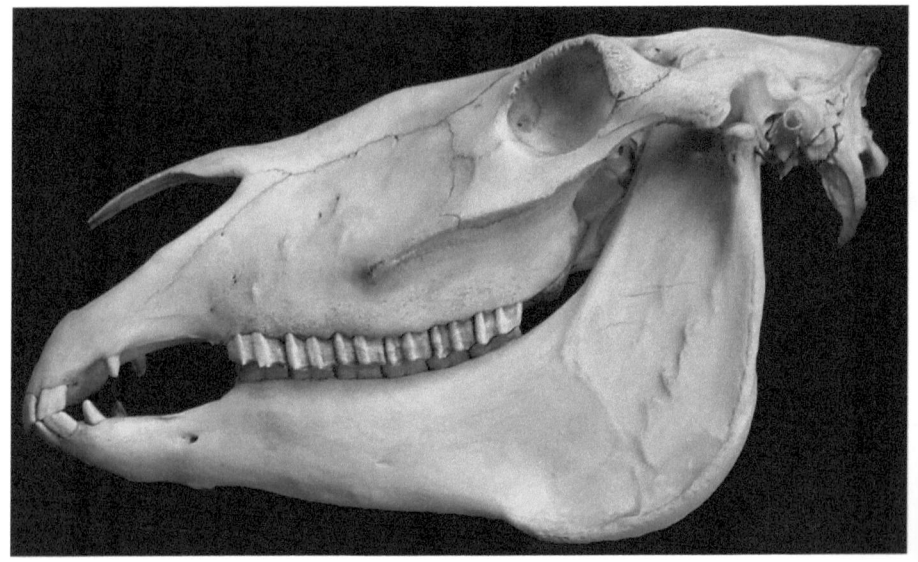

Anatomy of The Horses's Teeth

Types of Teeth, Age of Tooth Eruption, Common Dental Issues

The anatomy of horses' teeth plays a crucial role in their well-being. Horses are herbivores, a plant-eating species, and therefore have evolved to have teeth specializing in grazing and grinding plant material.

TYPES OF TEETH

1. **Incisors:** Horses have *12 incisor teeth.*
   - 6 on the top (maxilla) and
   - 6 on the bottom (mandible)

   The *incisors* are located at the front of the mouth and are used for cutting grass and other foliage.

   The *incisors* are flat rectangular and arranged in a curved arc called the *dental arcade.* The horse also uses his *incisors* for grooming and nibbling other herd members.

2. **Canine Teeth (Tushes):** These teeth are behind the *incisors.* Male horses have *4 canine teeth* between their corner incisor and molars. Mares have them, but they are usually not as developed, and

all four will not appear.

Canine teeth appear during the horse's 4th year of age

3. **Interdental Space:** Right after the *canine teeth*, there is a space before the back teeth, known as the "bar," or *Interdental Space*.

This space area is very sensitive and is where a bit would sit in the mouth, so we should be mindful if using a bit.

4. **Premolars and Molars:** Also known as the *cheek teeth*, located towards the back of the mouth. They too, are used for grinding and chewing plant material.

Adult horses typically have *12 Premolars and 12 Molars*, a total of *24 cheek teeth*.

The *premolars* are called "baby teeth" or "caps," and are deciduous teeth, meaning they eventually will fall out and will be replaced with *molars* as permanent teeth as the horse ages. The *molars* are larger and have distinct cusps that help grind food.

5. **Dental Arcade:** The arrangement of the teeth within the horse's mouth is referred to as the *dental arcade*.

The upper and lower teeth come together in a specific alignment to facilitate proper chewing and grinding of food.

Maintaining a balanced *dental arcade* is crucial for a horse's bite, digestion, and overall oral health.

6. **Continuous Tooth Eruption:** Horses have a unique dental characteristic called *hypsodont teeth*. This means their teeth continuously erupt throughout their lives, growing about 1/16th of an inch per year, naturally compensating for the wear caused by chewing tough forage. The grinding action of the teeth against each other gradually wears the teeth down, but the constant eruption from the jaw bone

ensures a relatively consistent tooth length.[1]

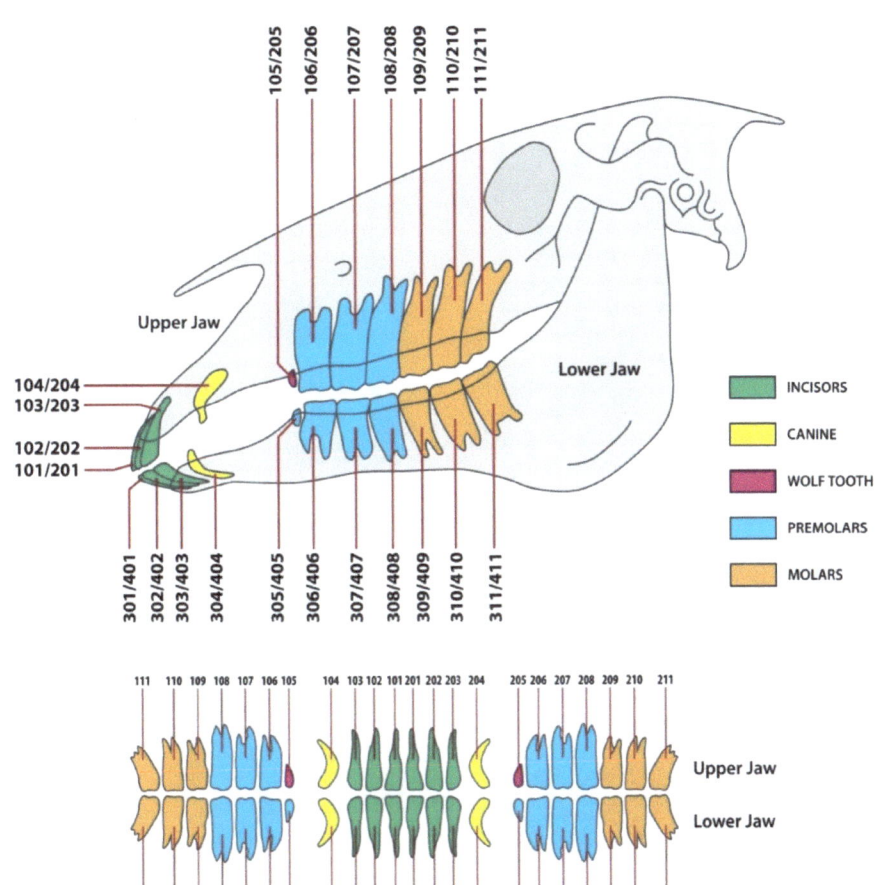

The Average Ages of Tooth Eruption in Horses

Deciduous (baby teeth)	Eruption Age
+1st incisor (centrals)	birth - first week
+2nd incisor (immediate)	4 - 6 weeks
+3rd incisor (corners)	6 - 9 months
+1st premolar +2nd premolar +3rd premolar	birth - 1st 2 weeks

Permanent	Eruption Age
+1st incisor (centrals)	2 1/2 years
+2nd incisor (immediate)	3 1/2 years
+3rd incisor (corners)	4 1/2 years
+Canine (bridle)	4-5 years
+1st premolar (wolf tooth)	5-6 months
+2nd premolar	2 1/2 years
+3rd premolar	3 years
+4th premolar	4 years
+1st molar	9-12 months
+2nd molar	2 years
+3rd molar	3 1/2-4 years

ESTIMATING AGE

An adult horse has 36 teeth: 12 incisors, 12 premolars and 12 molars. A foal will have 24 teeth: 12 incisors and 12 premolars. We estimate the age of a horse in four ways: The occurrence of permanent teeth, the disapearance of cups, angle of incidence and the shape and surface of the teeth.

Here are some key indicators to estimate a horse's age.

- **Eruption of Teeth:**

Deciduous (Baby) Teeth: Foals are born with or develop their first incisors within the first week. By nine months, they typically have all their baby incisors.

Permanent Teeth: Permanent incisors replace baby teeth starting around 2.5 years of age. The sequence usually goes central incisors, intermediate, then corners, finishing by around 4.5 to 5 years.

- **Wear Patterns and Tooth Shape:**

Infundibulum ("Cups"): These are deep indentations in the biting surface of the incisors.

The **Enamel Ring** or "mark" is the lower half of the infundibulum filled with cement after the "cup" has worn away. Its shape changes over time:

It transforms from oval (side to side) to triangular, then to round, and these changes can vary significantly between different horse breeds. In central incisors, the "mark" typically changes from oval to round between 5 and 12 years of age. The disappearance of the "mark" is highly variable, usually occurring between 12 and 18 years in the central incisors, and one to three years later in the intermediate and corner incisors.

Dental Stars: As the cups wear away, dental stars appear as a yellow-brown structure with dark lines or spots on the tooth surface, becoming more prominent with age. Dental stars typically appear in the central incisor at 5 years of age, the intermediate incisors at 6 years, and in the corner incisors at 7 to 8 years of age. As the horse ages, the dental star changes shape, becoming oval and then round, and moves toward the center of the tooth. By 15 to 18 years of age, the dental star is often the only structure visible on the chewing surface of the central incisors.

Tooth Shape Changes: The shape of the biting surface of the teeth changes from oval to round to triangular, and finally to biangular as the horse ages.

- **Galvayne's Groove:**

A vertical groove that appears on the upper corner incisor tooth. Between the ages of 9 to 10 years the groove typically first appears at the gumline. Between 18 to 20 years it extends progressively down the tooth, reaching the full length by this age range.

The Galvayne's groove is most useful for distinguishing between young and very old horses rather than determining precise ages.

ANATOMY OF THE HORSES'S TEETH

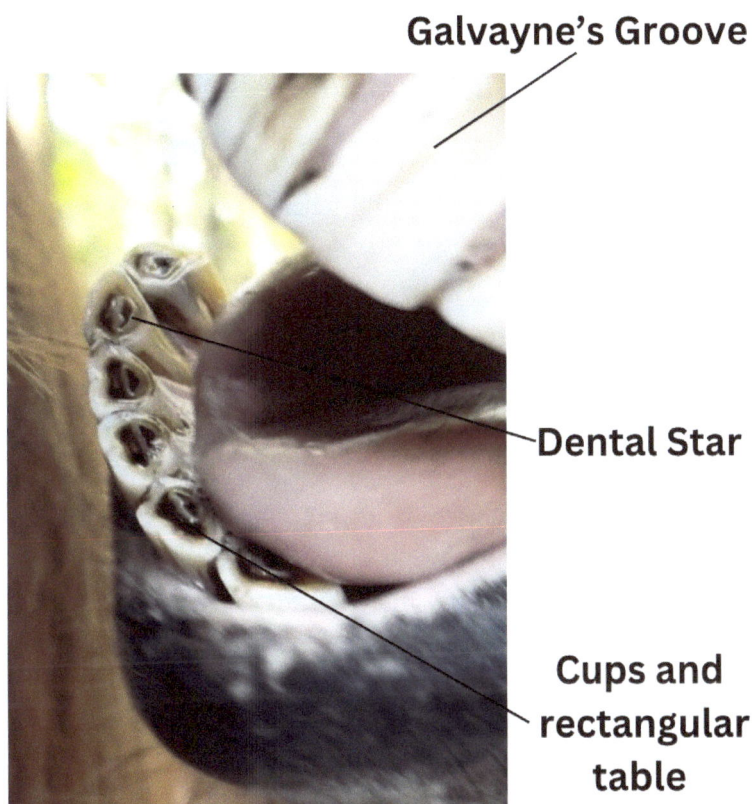

14 year old horse

- **Changes in Incisor Arcades:**

Young Horses: The upper and lower incisor arcades (the rows of teeth) align closely in a straight line when viewed from the side, forming an angle of about 180 degrees from the gum of the upper arcade to the gumline of the lower arcade.

As a horse ages, this angle becomes more acute, decreasing to around 120 degrees or less. This change is usually significantly noticeable around 20 years of age. The lower arcade tends to become more angled before the upper arcade.

The change in the angle of the incisor arcades helps in estimating a horse's age, especially in differentiating younger horses from older ones, though it provides a general indication rather than an exact age.

ANATOMY OF THE HORSES'S TEETH

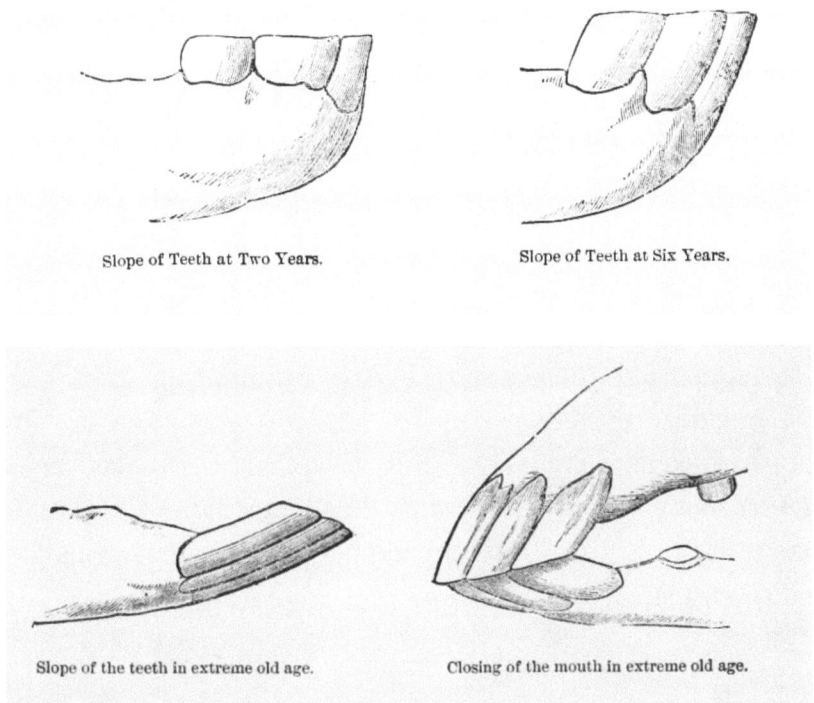

Slope of Teeth at Two Years.

Slope of Teeth at Six Years.

Slope of the teeth in extreme old age.

Closing of the mouth in extreme old age.

- **Length vs. Width of Upper Corner Incisor:**

In horses 5 to 9 years, the upper corner incisor is generally wider than tall. Around 9 to 10 years, it appears more square, and as the horse ages further, the tooth becomes taller than it is wide.

- **Presence of Hooks:**

Small projections or "hooks" can form on the back edges of the upper corner incisors around 7 years of age and may reappear at 11 to 13 years, though this is variable and not always reliable in determining age. [2]

Fifteen to 18 Years: All of the cups are gone. The central enamel rings (dental stars) are prominent, but small and round, and all the teeth are angular.

Twenty Years: Their is more length, angle and triangular surfaces of the teeth, and spaces may appear between the teeth.

Thirty Years: Dental stars appear dark, round and centered in the teeth. As wear progresses to the root changes appear in shape from oval to angular, and the Galvayne's Groove disappears. [3], [4]

These are general guidelines, and individual horses may vary due to factors like diet, enviornment, and genetics. For an accurate assessment, it's best to consult with a qualified equine veterinarian or dental specialist.

THE MOST COMMON DENTAL ISSUES

When adult horses eat, they naturally grind their food as they chew, repetitiously moving their jaw from side to side in a cyclical movement, grinding the whole top surface of the tooth and its edges.

Here are some common signs to determine if your horse needs to see a dentist:

1. **Quidding:** This is when you see the horse is dropping partially chewed grain or forage from their mouth.

2. **Periodontal Pocket:** This is caused by food getting trapped between the teeth and the gum line. The gum line recedes and creates a pocket that gets filled with bad bacteria that causes an infection.

3. **Step:** A *step* occurs when there is a missing cheek tooth or if one tooth is stronger than another. This will cause unevenness, where one tooth grows taller than another.

4. **Wave:** A *wave* is the differing heights of two or more different teeth in a row throughout the *premolars* and *molars*.

5. **Ramp:** This happens when the horse's lower jaw is slightly more forward than the upper jaw, affecting the first and last teeth of the *premolars* or *molars*.

6. **Hook:** The *hook* is the same as the *ramp*, but happens in the upper jaw.

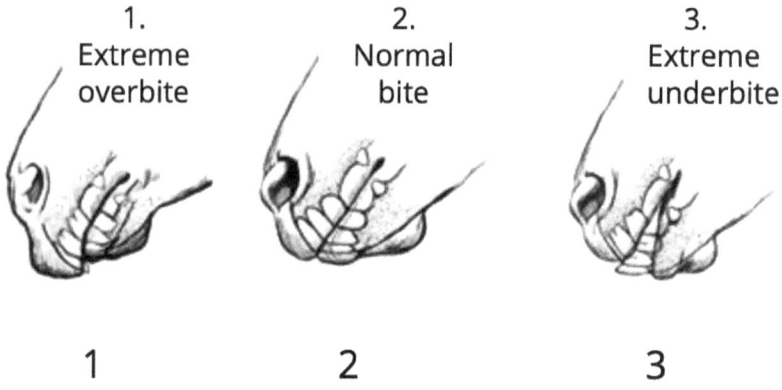

Proper dental care is essential for horses to maintain good health and to prevent future dental issues. Regular dental examinations by a qualified equine veterinarian or equine dental specialist are recommended to address any problems and maintain proper dental alignment and occlusion.[5, 6, 7, 8]

ANATOMY OF THE HORSES'S TEETH

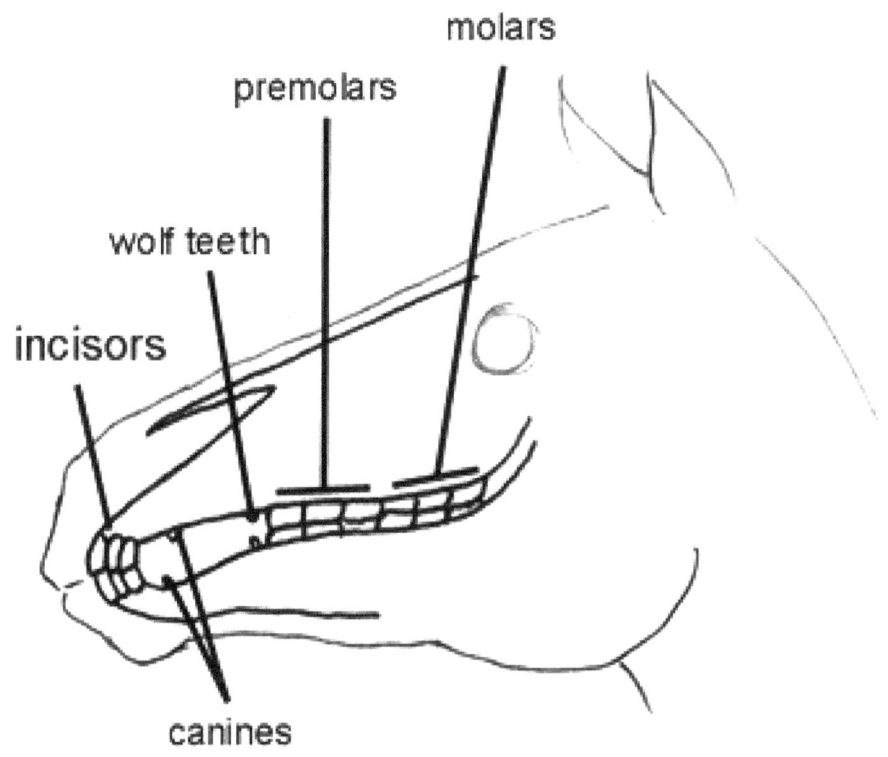

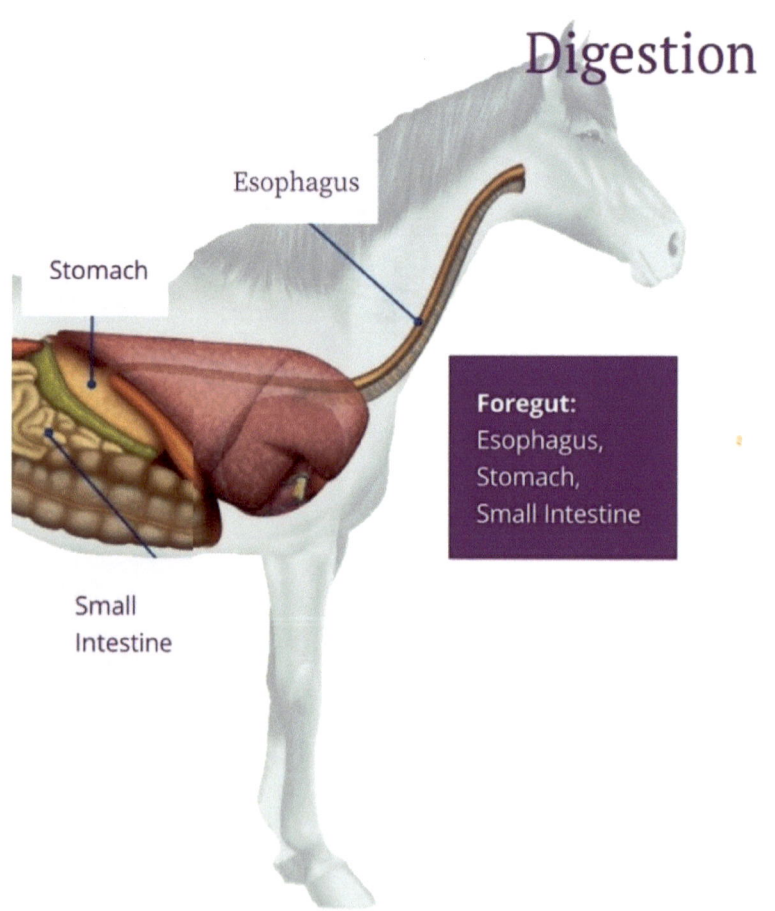

6

THE DIGESTIVE SYSTEM

THE HORSE'S STOMACH, TWO HALVES, TYPES OF ULCERS, SIGNS OF ULCERS, STARCH IN THE DIET, CONCLUSION

Horses are herbivores that naturally graze for approximately 19 or more hours a day, consuming plants, shrubs, and herbs. Their gastrointestinal tract starts with the *foregut*, consisting of the *esophagus, stomach,* and *small intestine.* When a horse chews its food, saliva is produced and swallowed, buffering the stomach acids. The horse's *stomach* is the smallest unit in the digestive tract, holding approximately 2-4 gallons, emphasizing the need for continuous grazing.

The food then leaves the stomach and enters the *small intestine.* The *small intestine* is approximately 70 feet long which comprises 30% of the total digestive system. Here, digestion and nutrient absorption occur through its three regions: the *duodenum, jejunum, and ileum.* Food moves swiftly through the small intestine, at about one foot per minute, and enters the *cecum* within 45 minutes of ingestion.

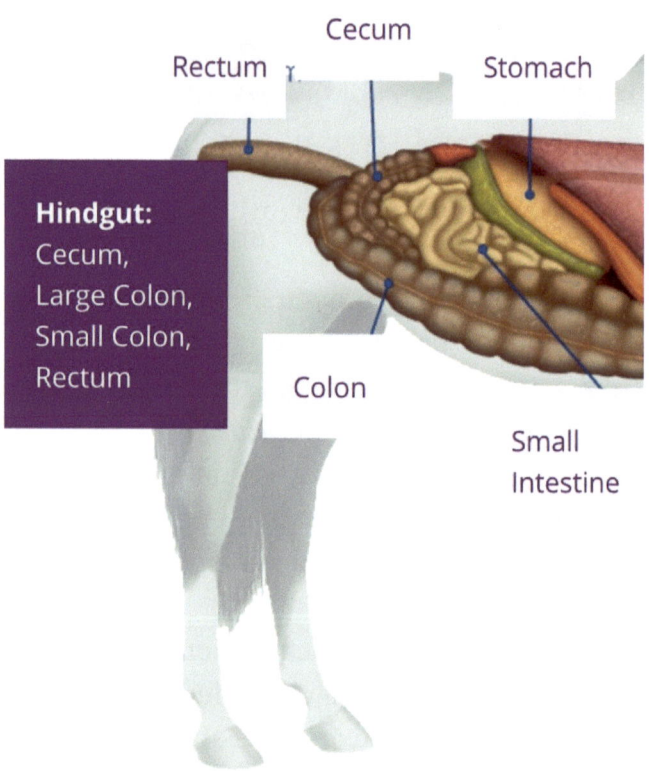

The *hind gut* consists of the *cecum, large* and *small colon,* and *rectum.*

The *hind gut* ferments the fiber from forage eaten, and is also responsible for water absorption. Forage is the energy source for the horse.[1]

THE HORSE'S STOMACH

~ TWO HALVES ~

The horse's stomach is made up of two halves. The lower stomach and the upper stomach.

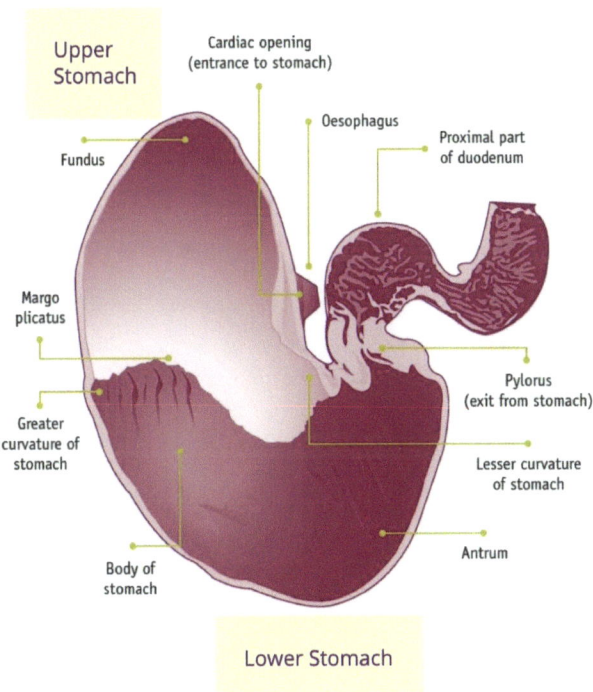

The Lower Stomach (glandular mucosa): A thick protective lining and continually produces over 6 cups of digestive acid an hour.

The Upper Stomach (squamous mucosa): A thinner lining with minimal protection, where most gastric ulcers form.

> *Ulcers* are intestinal sores that will not heal.

There are two types of ulcers:

    1. **Gastric Ulcers:** Form lesions on the stomach wall.

    2. **Colonic Ulcers:** Form in the hindgut, which is the colon.

Studies show that approximately 90% of all performance horses get ulcers, 60% of all horses in training, and 35-50% of pleasure horses.

A Horse's Stomach is Designed for Constant Foraging and Secretes Over
6 Cups of Gastric Acid Per Hour

A Horse Without Forage Can Develop Ulcers within 3 to 4 Hours

That is over 9 Gallons of Acid A Day!

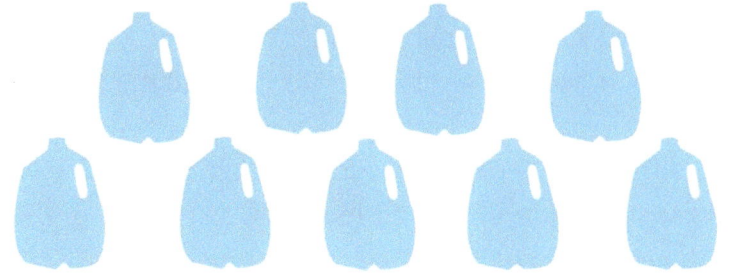

by Laura A Fitch

FACTORS AFFECTING DIGESTIVE HEALTH

Exercise increases gastric acid production and decreases blood flow to the gastrointestinal tract. Therefore, it's crucial for horses to have forage in their stomachs before exercising to minimize acid exposure to the upper lining.

Horses are designed for continuous foraging to neutralize gastric acid production with saliva. Diets high in starch from grains like oats, barley, corn, and milo can contribute to ulcer development by fermenting in the gastrointestinal tract, increasing acid levels. It's best to avoid feeding grains and opt for a high-roughage diet.

The horse's *stomach* secretes just over 6 cups of gastric acid an hour continuously every 24 hours. This is approximately *9 gallons of acid a day!*

> *Ulcers can develop within 3-4 hours* if left without forage.
> Horses are grazing animals and require a continuous intake of forage to prevent ulcers.

Stomach acid is produced to break down grass, hay and herbs, hence, the need for continual foraging. When the horse chews the hay and grass, it produces sufficient saliva to neutralize the gastric acid.

Horses are designed to graze, eating a high roughage diet of hay, grass and herbs. Grain diets high in *starch* contribute to the development of *ulcers*, due to the starch fermenting in the gastrointestinal tract, and creating even more acid. It is best not to feed any type of grains.

High stress from intense training, showing, shipping, stalling, exercise, and going for periods of more than 3-4 hours without forage, can lead to *gastric ulcers*.

SIGNS OF ULCERS

Signs of ulcers include: *picky* eating, depression, behavioral changes, recurring mild colic, poor appetite, chronic diarrhea, rough hair coat, and weight loss. Horses may also exhibit sensitivity when groomed or touched on their sides, and discomfort when girthed or saddled. They may nip, bite, or buck when being cinched, saddled, or ridden.

IMPACT OF STARCH IN THE DIET

Starch (carbohydrates), proteins, and fats and oils are digested by enzymes in the *small intestine* and absorbed.

Starch, digested in the *small intestine* turns into sugar, and grains like oats, barley, corn, wheat, and milo (sorghum), do not completely digest due to the grains' seed coat. The seed coat can pass through the *hind gut*. If this happens, bacteria quickly ferment it, causing *lactic acid* production and accumulation.

Lactic acid **accumulation:** Can cause *hind gut diseases* like colic, metabolic acidosis, laminitis, and founder.

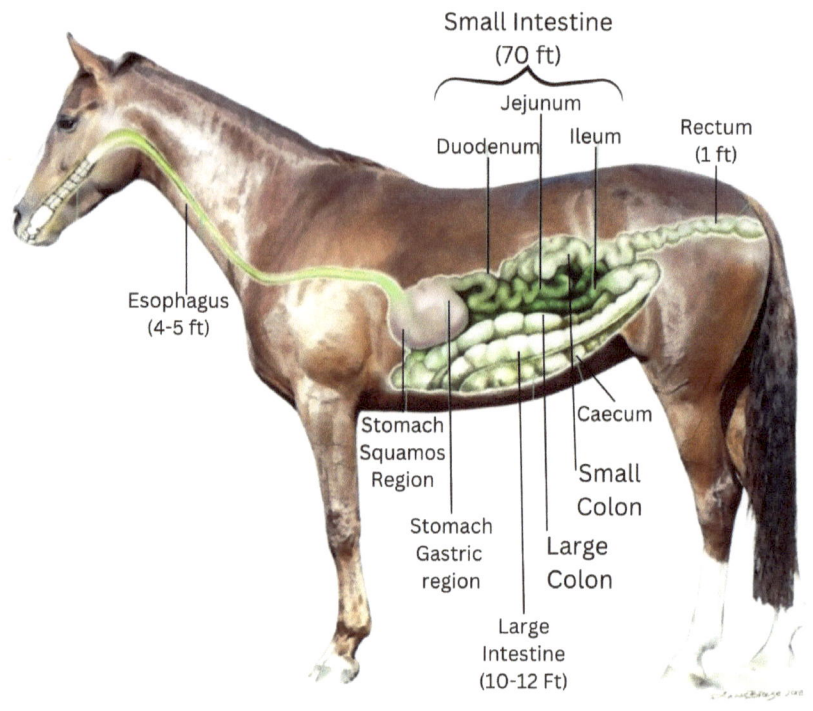

CONCLUSION

Excessive starch in the diet can contribute fermentation-related diseases such as colic, laminitis, founder, endotoxemia (inflammatory response), and metabolic disorders. It is crucial to prioritize forage in the horse's diet.

- **Forage Always:** Provide high-quality, low sugar forage with 24/7 access. Easy keepers or stalled horses should be provided

THE DIGESTIVE SYSTEM

with hay nets (preferably ground level hay pillows/nets to prevent eye injury and dust in the lungs) to control intake and ensure continuous foraging. The hay should last until turnout if stalled. 24/7 turnout is best.

- **Horses are grazing animals** and require continuous intake of forage to prevent ulcers.

- *Ulcers* **can develop within 3-4 hours.** Four hours without foraging equals over 24 cups of acid splashing around the stomach.

- **A Minimum** of 1.5% of hay for your horse's body weight should be fed daily. That's a minimum of 15 pounds of hay per 1000 pound horse. During winter months horses require increased hay intake to maintain warmth. This can be 15-30 pounds of hay a day or more to accommodate colder weather conditions.

- **Forage** is what keeps the horse's body warm in winter, not grain.

- **Do NOT feed grain**. Offer food-based vitamin/mineral balancers to meet the horse's nutrient requirements for a forage-based diet.

- **Feed small, frequent meals** less than 4-5 pounds per feeding of soaked hay cubes or hay pellets with supplements.

- **For performance horses**, lactating mares, and growing horses needing higher caloric intake, include highly digestible fibers and fats like flax, or chia seeds, hemp oil, coconut oil, rice bran, or water-soaked hay cubes.

If you are boarding your horse and your barn is feeding grain at mealtime, ask if you can provide your own vitamin/mineral supplement or water-soaked hay cubes for your horse's meals (water-soaking helps to prevent the horse from choking) in place of grain.

Choosing a fiber-rich diet over grains (starches) for your horse greatly reduces the risk of EGUS (Equine Gastric Ulcer Disease) and acidosis. It also improves digestion, body condition, behavior, immune functions, and performance.[2, 3, 4, 5, 6]

Use a hay net (preferably ground level hay pillows/nets to prevent eye injury and dust in the lungs) for easy keepers to prevent overeating, and for stalled horses to prevent and help heal stomach ulcers.

7

The Equine Hoof

Balance, Wall, Bars, Frog, Lateral Cartilage, Digital Cushion, Angles, Heels, and Trimming

The outer walls of a horse's hooves are made of a tough material called keratin, which continues to grow throughout the horse's life. Hooves do not contain veins or blood vessels and consist of three layers: the outer most layer, *(stratum externum)*, the middle layer *(stratum medium)*, and the innermost layer *(stratum internal)*.

The hoof wall, especially at the toe (front), is the thickest part of the wall and thins on average 50% out towards the quarters (sides) and heels. It, along with the bars and frog, bears the weight of the horse. The sole (bottom of the hoof) should not touch the ground when properly balanced.

Hoof Balance

A balanced hoof in a horse means that the forces pushing up from the ground are spread out evenly across the bottom of the hoof. Ideally, the point where these forces come together (like the center of balance) should line up with a specific point in the hoof to create a stable, even footing when the horse is standing or moving.

If the hoof is unbalanced, this alignment is off, causing one side of the hoof to bear more weight than the other. This uneven pressure can cause the hoof to sink unevenly into soft ground, leading to further imbalance and possibly discomfort or injury for the horse.

In practice, achieving this perfect balance involves more than just trimming the hoof evenly. The shape, position, and thickness of the hoof wall and sole also play a role, and these factors need to be considered to properly align everything for a balanced hoof.[1]

THE HOOF WALL

The hoof wall is a weight-bearing surface and therefore should be touching the ground all the way around the hoof. It's part of the horse's natural horse shoe. It can grow approximately 1/4 to 1/8th inch in one month. The horse should be on a regular trim schedule to keep a balanced hoof, most commonly 4-6 weeks.

Growth rates vary with age, faster in younger horses and influenced by nutrition and seasonal weather conditions. Horses with nutrition deficiencies grow weaker hooves, and weather conditions can cause hooves to grow slower, especially in the colder months. Tough terrain and housing conditions can cause the hoof to have more wear, while exercise creates blood circulation and promotes healthy hoof growth through improved blood circulation.[2]

Researchers from various fields, including medicine, mathematics, physics, and stem cell biology, have come together to better understand how the hooves grow, and why some hooves may develop abnormal shapes. They discovered that hoof growth starts from the coronet, and as the hoof material moves down, it gradually hardens into the tough outer layer we see, and in some cases the hoof wall grows in a curved manner rather than straight. This is linked to faster growth at the sides of the hoof (the quarters) compared to the front (the toe). They also found that heavier horses tend to have straighter hooves, while lighter horses might be prone to developing hooves

THE EQUINE HOOF

with a curved shape.[3]

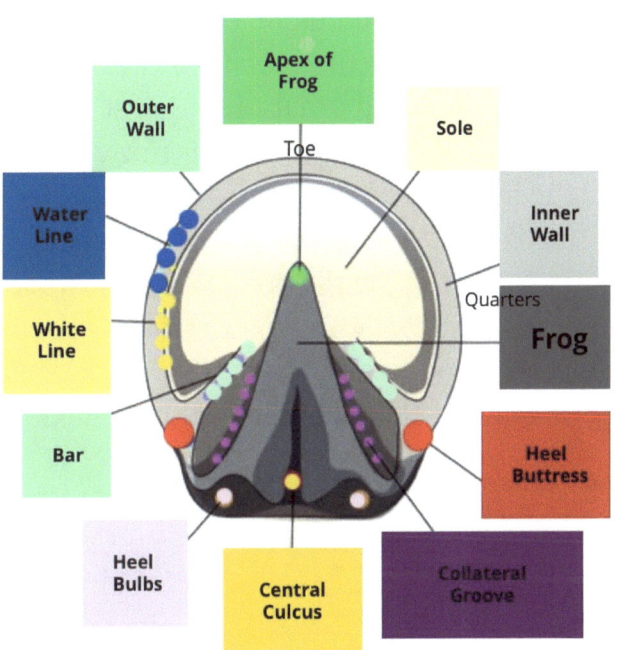

THE BARS

The bars are an extension of the hoof wall, running alongside the frog, stopping three-quarters of the way up the hoof wall and heel area, providing strength and support. They also contribute to the material that makes up the sole, controlling movement at the back of the hoof.[4]

THE FROG

The frog is an elastic V-shaped tissue covering the digital cushion of the foot. When it touches the ground, it presses on the *digital cushion*, flattening it, pushing it outward against the *lateral cartilage*, pushing the bars and wall apart, disbursing energy. Blood gets pumped from the hoof and up the leg by the pressure and change of the shape of the *frog* and *digital cushion*. The pressure and change of shape compress the veins in the hoof. When the hoof is lifted off the ground, the frog and its flexible outer structures return to their original shape, and blood flows back into the veins again. Exercise enhances the increase in blood flow and helps the hoof to grow.

LATERAL CARTILAGE

The thickness of the lateral cartilage plays a significant role in the strength of the hoof. It extends back and up from the inner and outer sides of P3 (third phalanx or coffin bone). Cartilaginous tissue surrounds and fuses with the *digital cushion* and envelops the blood vessels.

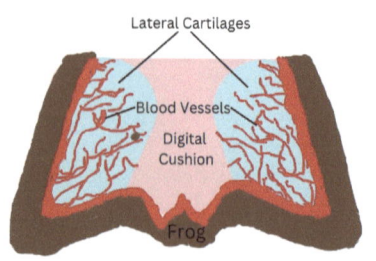

DIGITAL CUSHION

The *digital cushion* sits under the *frog* of the horse's hoof. Horses with thicker more *fibre-cartilaginous* (tough and flexible) structures, and more vascular structures have stronger hooves because they can disperse more of the impact to the hoof.

A horse with a long flat hoof and a low heel (under-run) will have a weaker hoof, or insufficient cartilage, and therefore dissipate the impact to the *navicular bone*, instead of the structures that are designed to take the impact.

New studies indicate that horseshoes on the horse lift the caudal foot off the ground and negate the horse's inner structures for shock absorption, creating a migration of the soft tissue structures.[5, 6]

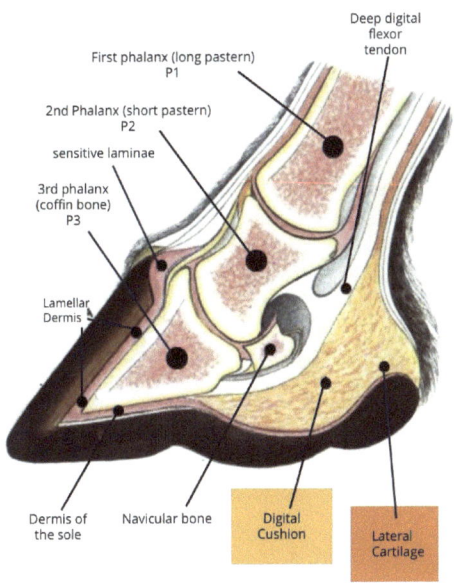

MEDIAL/LATERAL BALANCE

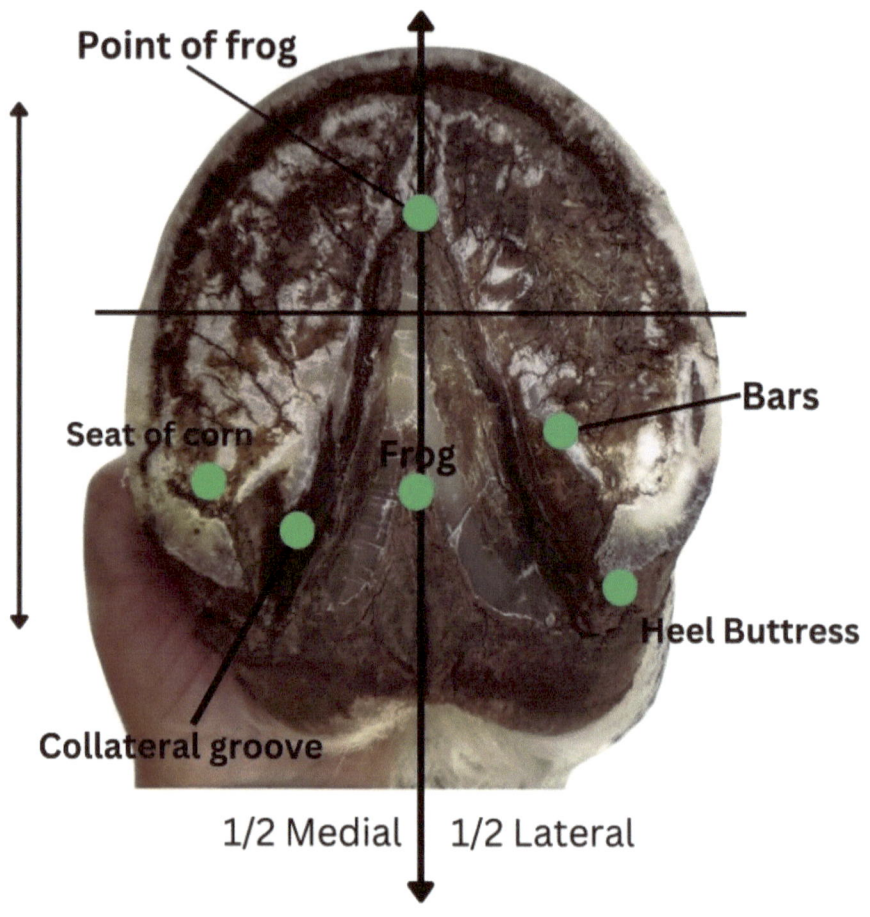

A balanced hoof will have equal equal medial/lateral size and shape.

ANTERIOR/POSTERIOR BALANCE

Anterior/posterior balance is approximately 1/2 forward and rear of the widest part of the hoof.

The balance in the lower leg bisect equally between the cannon bone, long pastern, and coffin bone, ensuring optimal alignment.

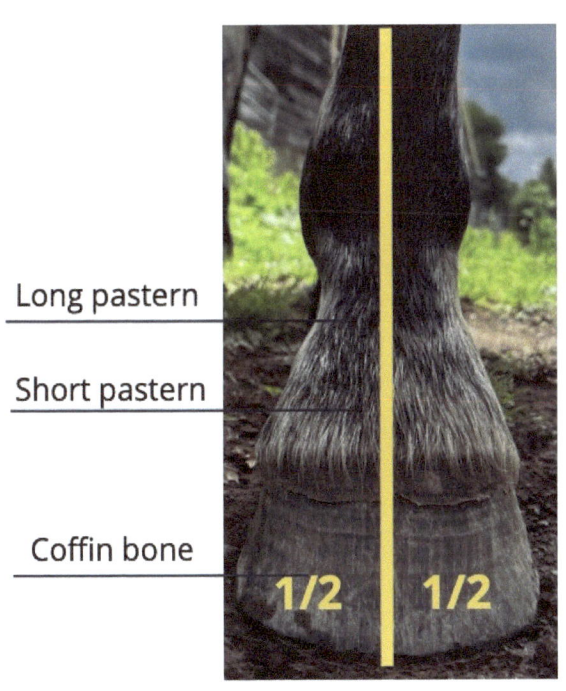

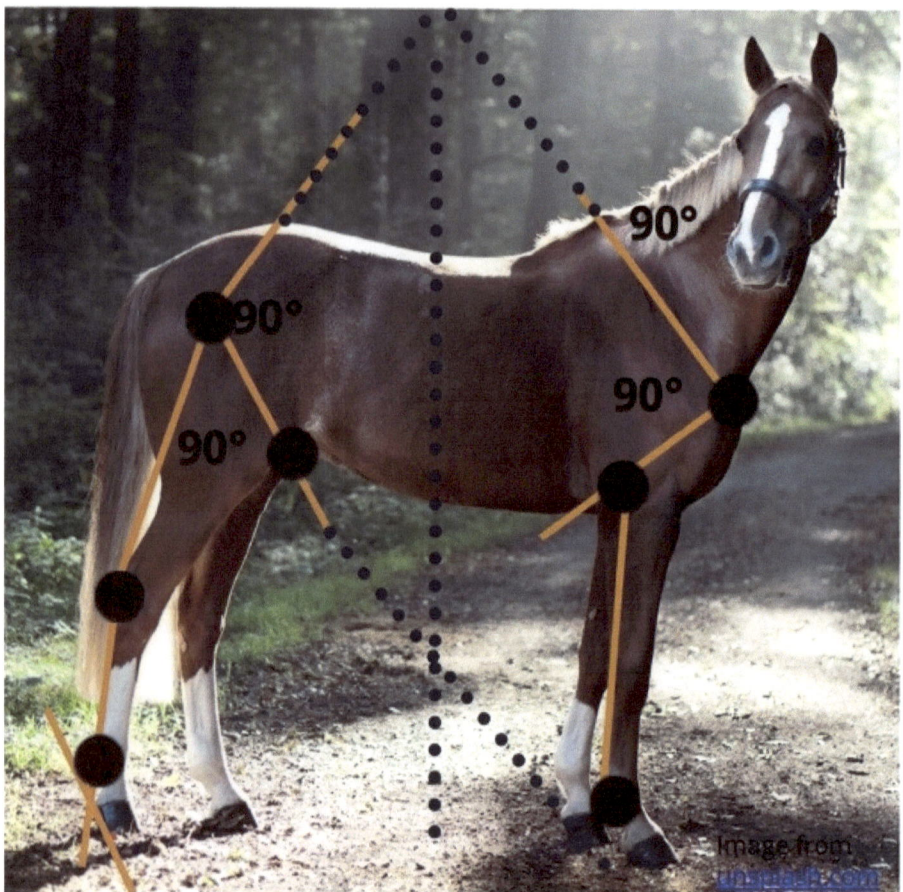

Proper trimming is critical for maintaining the horses's shoulder, pastern, and hoof angles.[7]

HOOF ANGLE

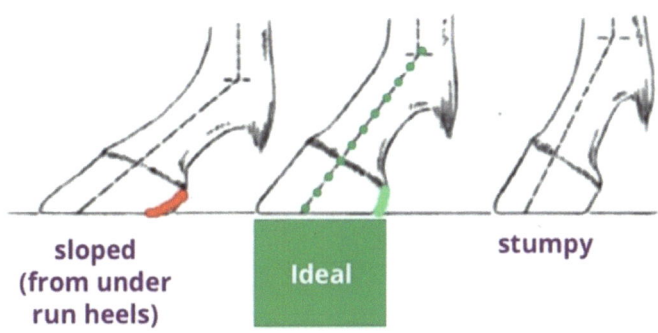

sloped (from under run heels) | Ideal | stumpy

Collapsed Heels/ Under Run/Caudal Failure

When the heel of a horse's hoof is too far forward, it causes *caudal failure*.

Collapsed heels can lead to a broken back hoof-pastern axis and negative palmer/planter angles.

Heels

Straight Heels + Widest Point + Correct Hoof Angles = Strong Hooves

For the hoof to work sufficiently, the heels should be straight down the walls at the highest widest part of the back of the hoof to bear the weight within the elastic modules. Straight heels trimmed at the hard sole plane evenly, at the highest widest point make for a strong hoof.[8]

Under-run heels is a hoof condition where the heel angle is more than 5 degrees lower than the toe angle, leading to a distorted hoof shape. This condition can range from mild to severe, with severe cases resulting in heel collapse due to damage to the hoof's structure. Appropriate trimming to restore the hoof angle is crucial to fixing the hoof.[9] Horses with under-run heels are predisposed to developing bruising, corns, abscesses, solar and wall separation, hoof cracks, sheared heels and other hoof problems if not properly managed.[10]

TRIMMING TO INTERNAL STRUCTURES

Trimming the hoof involves aligning the trim to internal structures, rather than blindly following a straight line from toe to heel. The collateral grooves serve as essential markers to understand the angles and location of these structures, guiding a more accurate trim.

- **Trim Heels:** Trimming heel walls almost level with the hard sole plane.

- **Collateral Grooves as markers:** The grooves provide insight to the angles and depth of the internal structures. Trimming should aim to follow the contours indicated by the grooves, avoiding over-thinning areas that are already too thin (e.g., the toe) and instead focusing on areas that are too thick (such as heels and bars).

- **Trimming parallel to internal structures:** Instead of trimming the hoof from heel to toe in a flat plane, the heel should be lowered in a way that follows the internal angles. Trimming parallel to the ground plane of the collateral grooves, helps preserve the integrity of the sole while correcting overgrowth.

- **Avoid excessive thinning**: If the sole at the toe is already thin, trimming heels in a straight line would exacerbate the problem. The goal is to balance the foot by addressing thick areas without compromising the already thin or structurally sound ones.

- **Tapering the bars:** The bars should be tapered to maintain concavity or relief at their ends, which can vary depending on terrain. These adjustments are crucial to ensuring optimal hoof function.

- **Regular re-evaluation:** Since the hoof's dynamics change over time, it's essential to re-evaluate at each trim and adjust based on wear patterns. The wear patterns provide insight into the horse's movement and informs necessary adjustments.

Summary: Trimming based on collateral groove depth and parallel to the internal hoof structures ensures that the hoof remains balanced, functional, and comfortable for the horse. This method prioritizes preserving the correct sole thickness and preventing toe-first landings or lameness due to improper trimming angles.[11]

8

A Guide To Parasite Prevention

Types of Worms, Parasite Management, How To Prevent Parasite Resistance

It's important to note that parasites are becoming resistant to a multitude of dewormers, and due to the resistance, it has become paramount that we test for parasites to determine the worm load our horses are carrying.

Horses should be tested at least twice a year for worms to determine if they are high shedders. The McMaster's Test is recommended and does fecal egg count parasites per gram of feces (EPG).

FECAL EGG COUNT

Worming is recommended if a fecal count is more than 200 eggs per gram (EPG).

- Mid-Range Shedder: 200-1,000 EPG

- High-Shedder: 1,000 EPG or more

*McMaster's Test does not detect Pinworms, Tapeworms, or Bots.

TYPES OF WORMS

Small Strongles: Also known as blood worms are the most common and most important parasite to manage in the adult horse.

These worms live on pasture grass, are eaten by the horse, then enter the horse's gastrointestinal tract, and exit through the feces. They can cause colic, anemia, diarrhea, weight loss, and poor performance in the horse.

Roundworms: (Ascarids) Transfer through the gut wall to the liver and through to the lungs. Larvae are then coughed up and swallowed. Heavy infestation can cause cough and nasal discharge as the worms travel in the lungs, and may cause weight loss and diarrhea.

Pinworms: Lay eggs on the outside of the anus, causing itching and scratching of the tail.

Tapeworms: Form into clusters between the *small intestine and large intestine*, causing digestive issues, colic, and fatal blockage.

Bots: Bot flies lay yellow sticky eggs on the horse's fur and tail. The horse ingests them by mouth, and they hatch into larvae and attach to the stomach lining to develop, exit in the feces, and pulsate into flies.

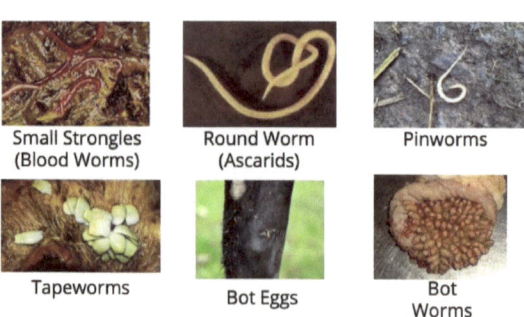

PARASITE MANAGEMENT

Since parasites are becoming resistant to deworming medications, Veterinarian medicine recommends manure and pasture management as the primary way to control parasites, along with laboratory testing. Pasture management reduces exposure to parasite eggs, and ensures that internal worm parasite burden numbers are at a minimum. Parasites are especially resistant to the dewormer Panacur, there is a large amount of documented resistance to the product.[1]

Internal parasites have an oral-fecal life cycle. After being ingested, adult parasites live in the horse's intestine, expelling eggs that are shed out in the feces. Cleaning your horse's pens, paddocks and pastures is crucial to parasite control. Composting the manure effectively kills parasite eggs, due to heat exposure. Eggs become non-viral at temperatures of 122-140 degrees Fahrenheit. This being said, parasite eggs can live for years on green pastures in the right conditions.

You can reduce your pasture contamination by identifying the high-shedding horses since they contribute up to 80% of you pasture contamination.[2,3,4,5]

A fecal egg count test will determine if your deworming protocol is working. If your horse has a fecal count of more than 200 EPG contact your veterinarian for a deworming protocol.

HOW TO PREVENT PARASITE RESISTANCE

- Only treat horses who need treatment. Those who have 200 EPG and above.

- Don't under dose your dewormer. Use a Weight Tape and add 10% for inaccuracies.

- Rest and rotate your grazing fields.

- Keep the same herd together in the same field for a few days after worming.

- Pick your grazing fields daily to remove manure.

- Keep your picked manure pile away from your grazing fields.

- Keep all new horses separated until they're tested.

- Don't let your horse graze at horse shows or events. They are loaded with parasites from other horses. Bring hay from home, instead of letting your horse graze.

- Use resistance testing to be sure your wormer is working.

- The dewormer Panacur has been documented and found to be highly resistant to parasites.

- Compost your manure to kill parasites.

- Cross-grazing with sheep or cattle can keep horse parasite numbers down. They are not a host for your horse's parasites.

- Keep your stables, shelters, water troughs, and buckets clean to prevent your horse from ingesting eggs.

> *When you test and deworm, wait two weeks and retest. If the test results have not reduced at least 85%-95% then the worms are resistant to the dewormer you used.[6]

De-worming a horse does not provide long-term protection against future worm infections. If a horse grazes on a pasture contaminated with infective strongle larvae, re-infection can begin immediately. Most de-wormers only eliminate adult worms in the digestive system, while some newer medications also target encysted stages of small strongyles before they emerge and start laying eggs. These newer drugs can extend the period during which the horse doesn't pass eggs, providing additional, but temporary, protection. However, larvae outside the digestive tract are largely unaffected, and newly developed adult worms can thrive until detected through egg production, prompting another round of de-worming.[7]

9

THE BEST SLEEP PRACTICES

Two Stages of Sleep, Signs of Sleep Deprivation, Identifying The Root Cause

Horses have many various living arrangements, whether they are stalled or out in the field 24/7. It's crucial that horses can rest adequately during the day or night to get proper sleep.

TWO STAGES OF SLEEP

The horse experiences two stages of sleep:

1. **Non-Rapid Eye Movement (NREM)**
2. **Rapid Eye Movement (REM)**

During a typical sleep episode, a horse cycles through stages such as wakefulness, REM sleep, and NREM sleep. On average, a horse requires 3-5 hours of sleep per day, sleeping intermittently throughout.

Research indicates that a horse spends approximately 2.98 hours per day in NREM sleep and the remaining time in REM sleep, totaling about 3.85 hours daily on average.

> It's important to note that horses *must lie down* to achieve REM sleep, which is a deeper sleep than NREM. Horses that do not lie down for REM sleep may suffer from a deficiency that can adversely affects their health and well-being.

Horses typically exhibit certain behaviors before sleeping, such as, circling, yawning, blinking, eye twitching, or paddling. If a horse remains standing during REM sleep due to the loss of muscle tone its legs may buckle or it may collapse. Therefore, It's essential to provide a flat, dry area sheltered from the elements where the horse can lie down comfortably, whether in a stall or outdoors.[1]

SIGNS OF SLEEP DEPRIVATION

A horse that does not get enough sleep may experience sleep deprivation. A horse can be sleep-deprived for up to two weeks before showing any signs. The clear clinical sign of sleep deprivation is when a horse appears drowsy during the day, fails to lie down, and may experience partial collapsing and regaining footing. If your horse is drowsy during the day, not lying down, and having collapsing episodes, these are all signs of a sleep-deprived horse.[2]

IDENTIFYING THE ROOT CAUSE

It is crucial to identify why a horse may not be getting adequate sleep. Several factors could contribute to this:

Environment: Is the horse comfortable and safe in its environment? Does it get along with herd mates, or are their conflicts? If stalled, are herd mates in the stalls next to him or are they separated?

THE BEST SLEEP PRACTICES

Are neighboring stalled horses a source of stress? Is the stall or pen sufficiently large enough for the horse to lie down and stretch out comfortably? Is their at least 6 inches of clean dry bedding in the stall or shelter for the horse to lie down and stretch out comfortably?

> A study showed that horses provided only 2 inches of bedding in their stalls experienced less REM and NREM sleep and spent significantly more time standing, indicating sleep deprivation. Horses slept significantly better with 6 inches of bedding.[3]

Environmental Factors: The environment can greatly affect the quality and duration of sleep for the horse. Consider noise levels, lighting, travel, showing, changes in handlers, losing a herd mate, solitary living, extreme temperatures, injuries, arthritis, pain, or changes in herd dynamics, or living situation.

Consulting with a veterinarian can help identify the root cause of a horse's sleep deprivation.

RESOLUTION

Once the cause for sleep deprivation is addressed and the horse can sleep comfortably, it's beneficial to allow the horse some time off. Initially, the horse may sleep for extended periods for the first couple of days, to compensate for lost sleep.[4]

Part III

The Horse Owner's Guide To Tack Fitment

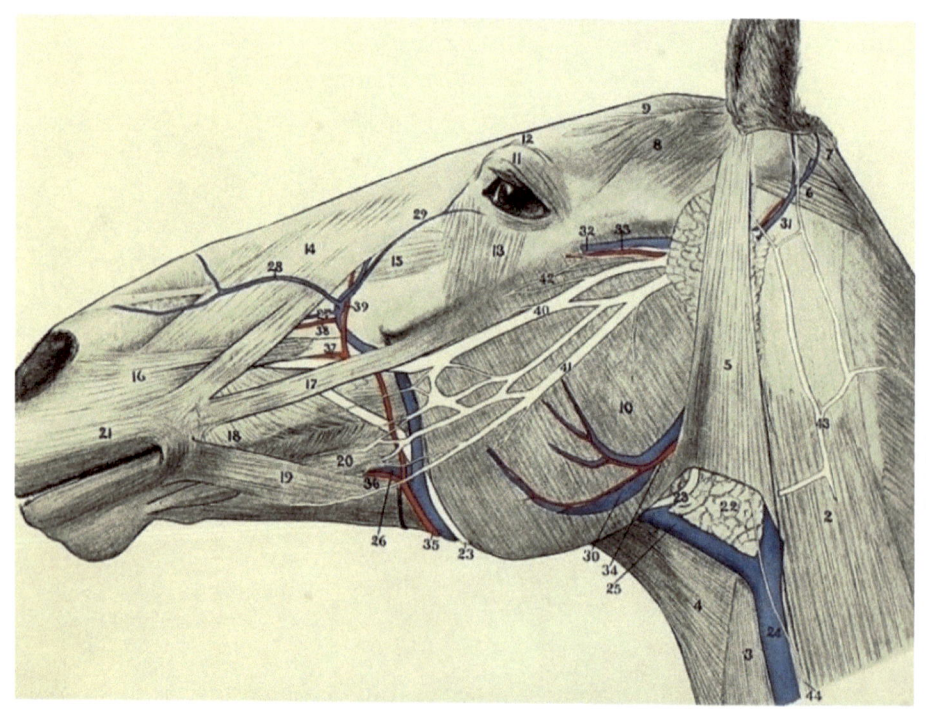

Bridle and Halter Fitting Guide

Cranial Nerves, Bridle and Halter Fitment, Facial and Ear Hair Rules

Knowing the placement and functionality of the horse's cranial nerves is of utmost importance for correctly fitting a halter and bridle.

The horse's *cranial nerves* originate in the brain. There are 12 pairs of cranial nerves, one set for each side of the horse's head. The cranial nerves can either have *sensory fibers* or *motor fibers*.

The 12 pairs of cranial nerves of the horse are:

1. **CN I Olfactory Nerve:** A sensory nerve, for smells that enter the nasal cavity.

2. **CN II Optic Nerve:** A sensory nerve that carries messages from the retina to the brain where vision is interpreted.

3. **CN III Oculomotor Nerve:** A motor nerve, part of a group of nerves responsible for supplying nerves to the head.

4. **CN IV Trochlear Nerve:** These are motor nerves that enable chewing.

5. **CN V The Trigeminal Nerve:** The fifth cranial nerve is re-

sponsible for the three branches along the *cavernous sinus* to the orbit of the eye. The *maxillary nerve* is a sensory nerve that goes to the teeth. This is the nerve the veterinarian will perform a nerve block to perform a dental extraction when standing, and the *mandibular nerve* is a mixed nerve along the medial side of the mandible and supplies all the nerves to the dental arcade. They are nerves responsible for the sensations of the face and motor functions such as biting and chewing.

6. **CN VI The Abducens Nerve:** This is a motor nerve controlling the lateral movement of the muscles of the eyeballs.

7. **CN VII The Facial Nerves:** Are made up of both sensory and motor fibers, supplying the ear canal, salivary glands (parasympathetic control), lacrimal glands, nasal cavity, muscles of facial expression and palate, and sensory input from the tongue for taste.

8. **CN VIII The Vestibulocochlear Nerve:** The eighth pair of sensory cranial nerves from the organs of hearing and balance in the inner ear of the brain. This nerve branches in two, the *vestibular nerve*, which is resposible for balance, and the *cochlear nerve, responsible for hearing.*

9. **CN IX The Glossopharyngeal Nerve:** This is part of the *vagus nerve group*, and is both a sensory and a motor nerve resposible for swallowing, tongue movement, and sensation.

10. **CN X The Vagus Nerve:** This is made up of mixed fibers known as the *inflammatory nerve,* that runs through the crural region of the horses' *diaphragm.* 80% of the vagus nerve fibers communicate from the body to the brain, and 20%

of the fibers communicate from the brain to the body. The *diaphragm* has fascial and neurological connections that have body-wide implications.

11. **CN XI The Accessary Nerve:** or the *Spinal Accessory Nerve*, is a motor fiber providing motor control for the movement of the horse's neck.

12. **CN XII The Hypoglossal Nerve:** This is mainly a motor nerve, that controls intrinsic and extrinsic muscles of the tongue.

The cranial nerves most affected by the bridle fit are the *Trigeminal Facial*, and *Glossopharyngeal Nerves*. It is essential to have a proper fitting bridal so as not to cause facial paralysis, reduced blood flow, or reduced airflow for breathing.[1,2]

Facial nerve paralysis in horses is a condition where the nerves controlling the ears, eyelids, lips, and nostrils are damaged. This leads to visible drooping on one side of the horse's face, and the affected side may lose muscle tone. The muzzle might pull toward the unaffected side, and the horse may struggle to blink properly, which can cause eye problems like corneal ulcers.

The most common cause is when a horse lies on its side for too long, pressing its face against the ground or a halter, especially if there are metal parts on the halter. Other causes include direct injuries, fractures in the skull, or certain diseases.

FACIAL NERVE PARALYSIS

Facial nerve paralysis is quite common in horses. It is a condition where the nerves controlling the ears, eyelids, lips, and nostrils are damaged. This leads to visible drooping on one side of the horse's face, and the affected side may lose muscle tone. The muzzle might pull toward the unaffected side, and the horse may struggle to blink properly, which can cause eye problems like corneal ulcers.

The most common cause is when a horse lies on its side for too long, pressing its face against the ground or a halter, especially if there are metal parts on the halter. Horses should not wear halters when they are loose out in the pasture or unattended. Other causes include direct injuries, fractures in the skull, or certain diseases.

Treatment usually focuses on managing symptoms, like using eye ointment to protect the affected eye and giving anti-inflammatory medications. If the paralysis is caused by pressure from lying down, it often improves within a few days. The outlook depends on how severe the injury is; in some cases, the horse may only partially recover over time.[3]

Researchers studied bridle nosebands, the strap that goes around the horse's nose. Tightening the noseband too tight can make the horse uncomfortable and even in pain. Tight nosebands can clamp the horse's jaw shut, which can cause the inside of their mouths to press against their sharp teeth, leading to pain. The common advice is to be able too fit two fingers between the horses noseband and face. However, this guideline isn't very precise, people have different finger sizes. Researchers also found that tighter nosebands increased the temperatures in the horses eyes and skin, which can be a sign of pain and discomfort.[4]

BRIDLE AND HALTER FITTING GUIDE

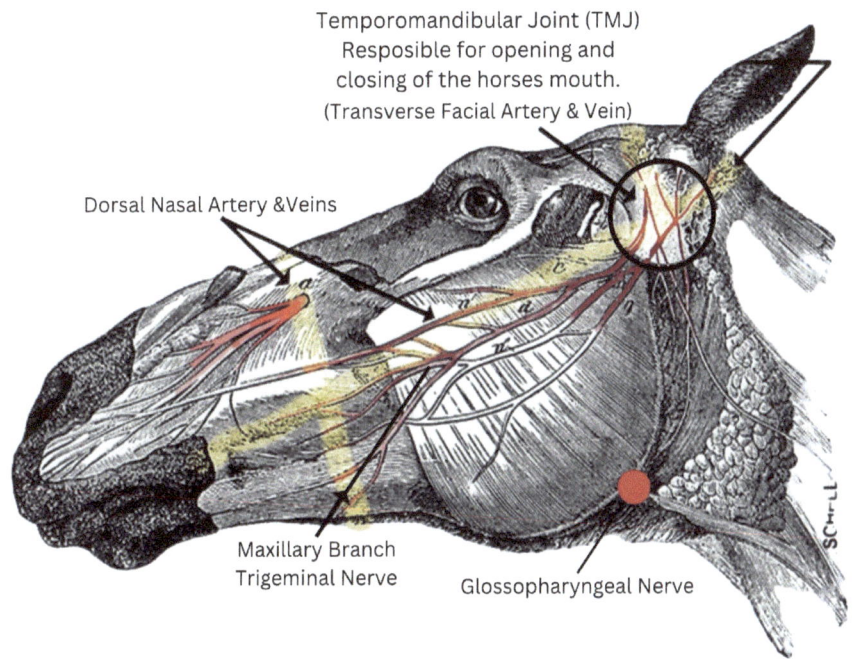

In 2023 the French FEI (International Equestrian Federation) implemented a standardized gauge measuring the space between the head and the bridle noseband at 1.5 cm. Stating, every single horse will be checked before entering the show arena.

BRIDLE FITTING GUIDE

You should be able to fit at least two vertical fingers under the browband. If too tight it causes pressure on the ears and poll.

You should be able to fit a minimum of two vertical fingers under your noseband. It is recommended you are able to fit your hand through.

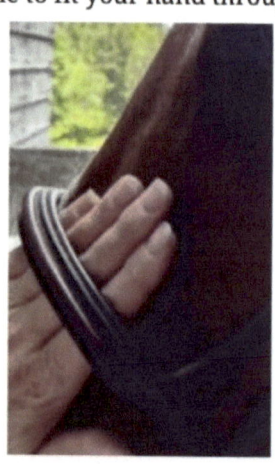

The buckles should sit on or around eye level.

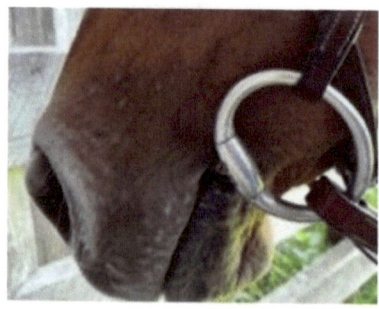

There should be NO wrinkles in the upper lip for proper bit fit.

BRIDLE AND HALTER FITTING GUIDE

Be sure to have good ear clearance on the head piece so the horse can move ears freely

The browband should be placed two vertical finger widths below the ear and above the TMJ

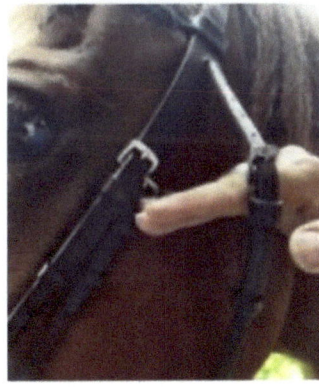

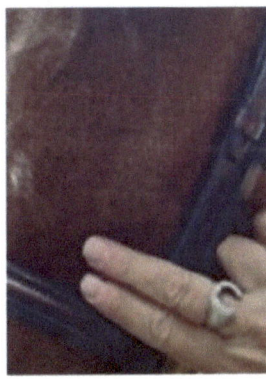

Your throatlatch should be done loosely so the horse can bend and lengthen without restriction.

The noseband should sit 1-2" below the cheek bone.

HALTER FITTING GUIDE

The halter's nosepiece should fit above the *nasoincisive notch*, which is the indentation above the horse's nostrils, where the face's soft tissue meets the nose bone.

The nasal bones are thin and delicate, and any pressure can result in a fracture. The halter should also fit below the cheekbones (facial crest) on either side of the horse's face.

FACIAL HAIR

It's important to note that horses heavily depend on their long and sensitive whiskers to ensure their safety. The whiskers function as a sensory organ vibrating in response to different tactile stimuli and relaying this information to the brain. This aids in the horses spatial awareness, object detection, and safe exploration of their enviornment by detecting subtle changes in pressure and texture. By sensing air movements caused by nearby objects, horses can avoid collisions and safeguard themselves from being at a considerable disadvantage to their survival and overall health. They could be in jeopardy without their whiskers. [5]

A horse's whiskers grow around the upper and lower lip, and eyes. Research suggests they provide the horse with information to determine the distance of objects from their mouth and eyes to protect them from injury. The hairs sense objects on the ground and in front of the horse's eyes, where the horse's monocular vision has the blind spot in front of them.

EAR HAIR

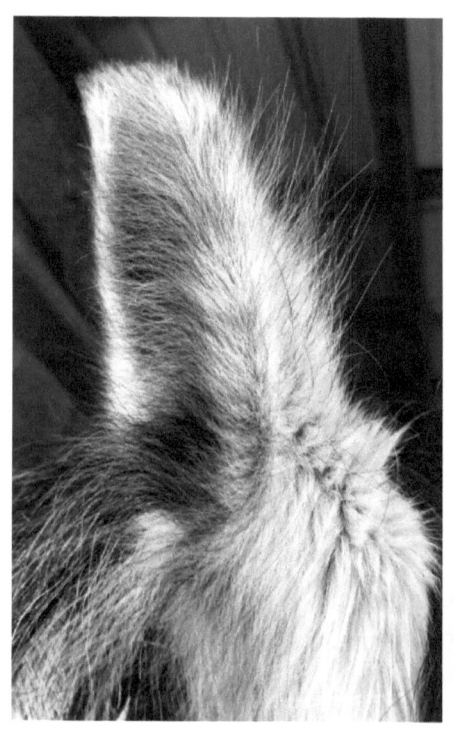

Equestrian organizations not only prohibit trimming a horse's whiskers, eyebrows, and eyelashes, for protection from injury, but they also prohibit clipping the horses's ear hair inside the ear.

The horse's ear hair protects the delicate structures of the inner ear, and the hairs inside and around the ear protect the ears from biting bugs, and prevent dirt and debris from entering the ears. Ear hair gets thicker like the rest of the horse's winter coat, protecting the ears from frostbite in freezing temperatures.[6]

CONCLUSION

Trimming a horse's whiskers, eyebrows, eyelashes, and ears can have serious consequences for the horse's health and well-being. Trimming may cause confusion, stress and increased risk of injury, as well as, irritations and infections. Trimming also affects the horse's ability to sense its surroundings, and stay warm during the colder months. Moreover, many equestrian competitions have strict rules against trimming horse's whiskers, eyebrows, and eyelashes, and doing so can lead to disqualification from competing. Therefore, it is generally not recommended to trim these hairs unless it is necessary for medical reasons.[7]

Whisker trimming has been banned by the FEI, British Dressage, British Eventing, German, French and Swiss National Equestrian Federation, and other organizations as well.[8,9]

EQUINE BONE FUSION SKELETAL TIMELINE

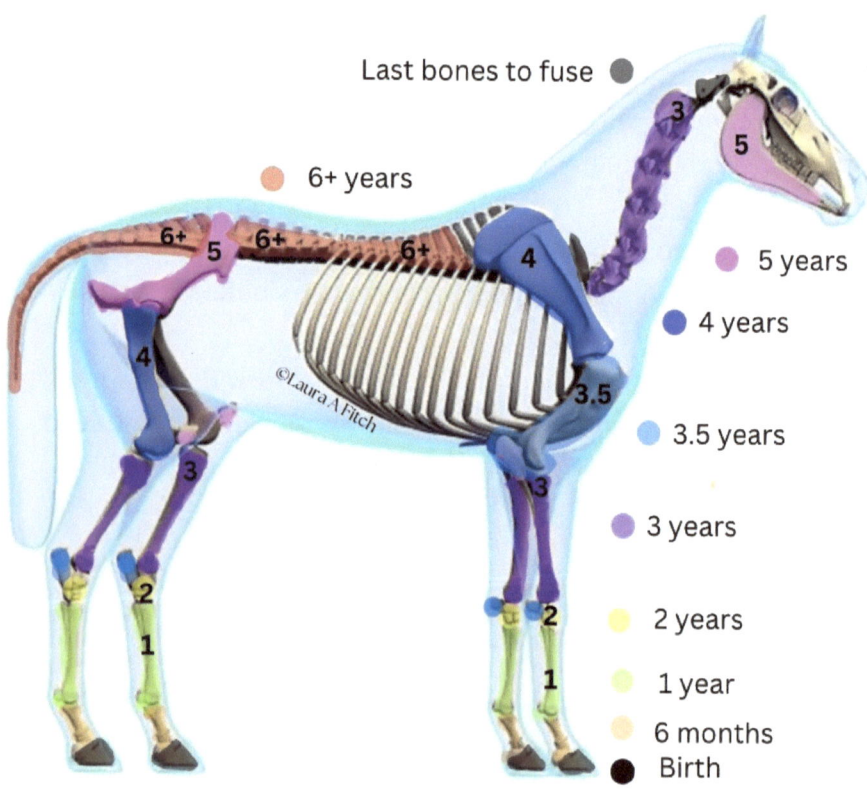

DISCLAIMER: This timeline is approximate, some horses may require more time for bone fusion,.

II

Saddle Fit

How-To-Guide, Skeletal Maturity, Saddle Fit for The Horse and Rider, Fitting a Breastplate, Measuring The Rider for Saddle Fit

Skeletal Maturity

There is much debate over when to start riding or training a horse, which should ideally be based on skeletal developmental timing. As a horse matures, the growth plates gradually ossify and close, indicating the end of bone growth.

The horse's bones fuse from the bottom up, with the lower bones fusing first and the upper bones last. A horse is not fully mature until approximately 6 years of age, with the back being one of the last parts to fully mature. By two years of age, a horse will reach 98% of its mature height.

Exercise is beneficial for horses as it supports and strengthens the development of the muscular-skeletal system. However, excessive exercise, and stalling can lead to a range of bone and joint abnormalities associated with the skeletal growth processes of the horse.[1,2]

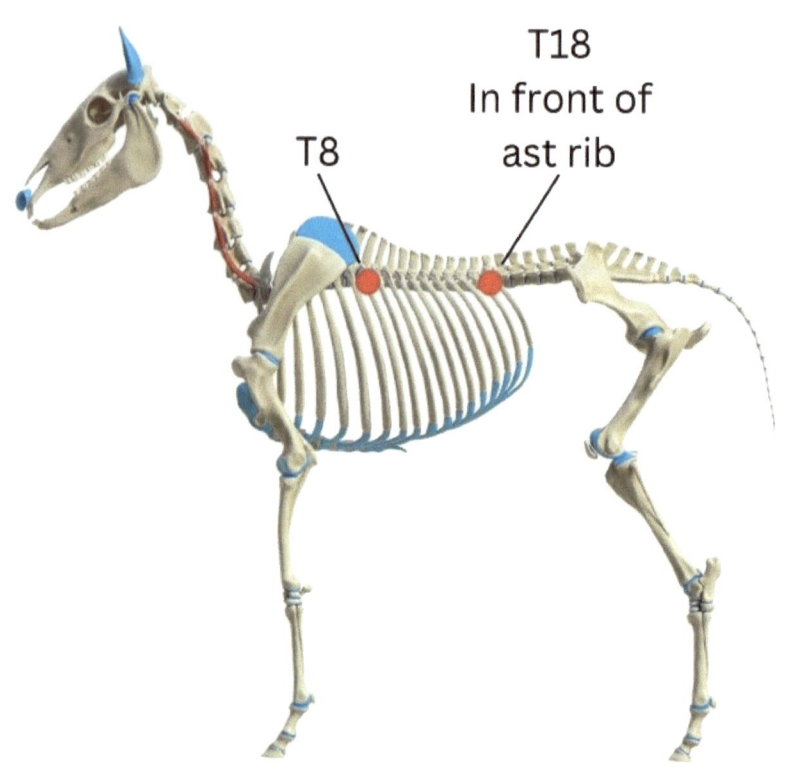

The saddle sits between thoracic vertebrae T8 which is two finger widths behind the scapula, and T18, in front of the horse's last rib.

SADDLE FIT FOR THE HORSE AND RIDER

Correct saddle fit for the English and Western saddles is most important for the comfort of the horse's muscles, joints, and well-being.

The english saddle should fit *between* the 8th thoracic vertebrae, and the thoracic vertebrae T18.

Thoracic vertebrae T8 can be found by placing two fingers width behind the back of the scapula, and upwards towards the top of the withers. Thoracic vertebrae T18 is the last rib at the back of the horse. Once you find the last rib, slide your hand up at an angle to the top of the horse' back. The saddle should fit *inside* these two perimeters, T8 and T18.

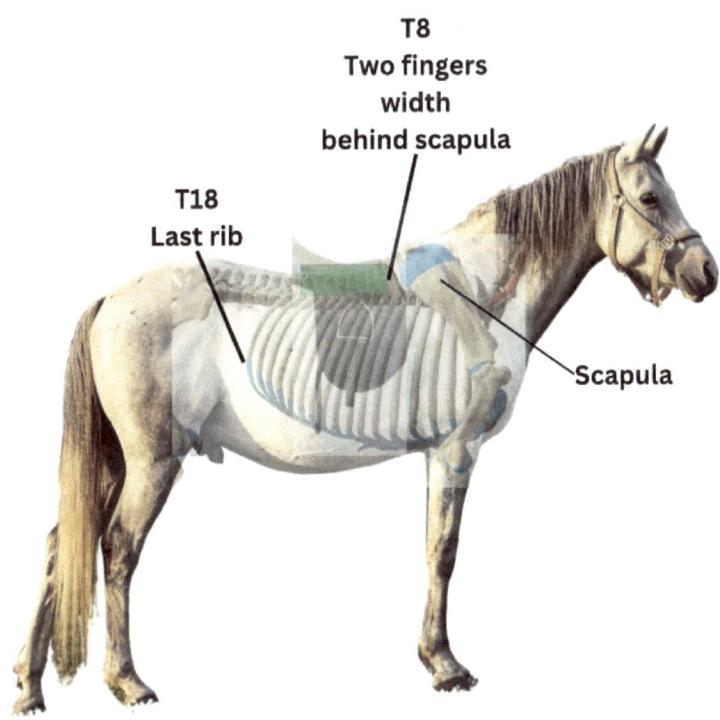

When doing a saddle fit, it is best to put the saddle on without a saddle blanket or pad. Then find the saddle tree points on the front of the saddle. They lie between the two nails at the front of the saddle and should land at the point of T8 on the horse's back. The saddle should sit at least *two fingers width behind the horse's scapula,* allowing the scapula to have swinging movement.[3]

The saddle tree points lie between the two nails

SADDLE FIT

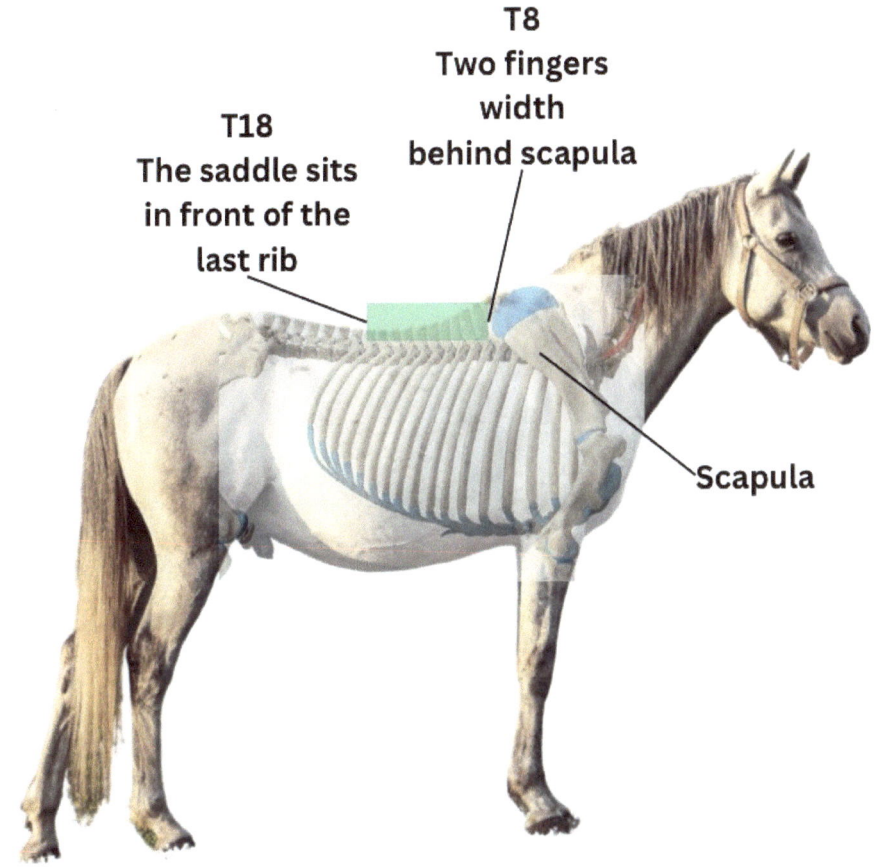

T8
Two fingers width behind scapula

T18
The saddle sits in front of the last rib

Scapula

The Back of the saddle should be in front of the T18 point. If you go past vertebrae T18, the saddle will be sitting on the horse's kidneys.

The *width* of your saddle can be determined by how level the saddle sits in the horse. Draw an imaginary line from the front of the saddle to the top of the rear of the saddle. It should be level from front to back. If it is level the *saddle width* is correct.

If the saddle runs downhill to the front of the saddle, it is too wide, and the saddle will be putting pressure on the horse's withers. You should be able to fit 3 stacked fingers between the withers and the lowest part under the gullet. If the tree is too wide the saddle will rock front to back. Allow 2 fingers to fit on either side of the pommel by the withers to allow the horse to turn left and right comfortably.[4]

SADDLE FIT

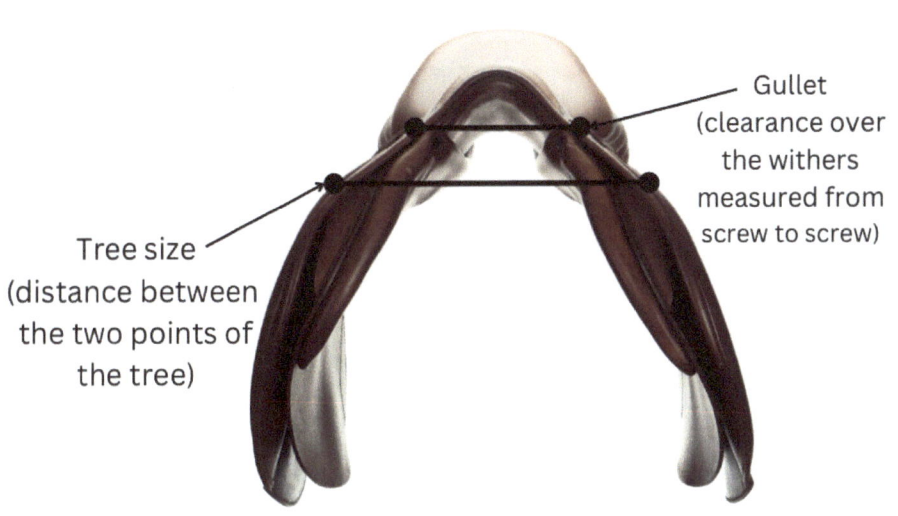

Tree size (distance between the two points of the tree)

Gullet (clearance over the withers measured from screw to screw)

Look and feel under the saddle to check that the panel of the saddle lays evenly on the horse and is touching the horse from front to back. There should be no gaps. Gaps in the saddle in the middle of the horse's back are called *bridging*.

The deepest part of your saddle should be in the middle of the saddle between T8 and T18. English jumping saddles have a *forward flap*, and cover more of the horse's scapula, but the flap is flexible and moves with the horse's shoulder. Also, be sure your saddle isn't too short or uphill, the rider's balance will be off and cause the rider to sit too far back in the saddle making it ride forward.[5]

The Western Saddle

The western saddle standards of fitting are almost identical to the fitting of the English saddle. The western saddle bars are 2 finger widths behind the scapula, but the back of the saddle will extend over the loins of the horse. The rider should be positioned, sitting at the center of the saddle, which is the deepest point of your saddle's seat, and the deep point of the seat should be in front of the points of the *cantle*.

Your stirrups should hang directly below the point of the *cantle*. The underneath of your saddle should be smooth, with no lumps or bumps, or protrusions where the conches, screws, nails, or strings are attached. Check that the saddle makes full even contact with the horse and that there in no *bridging* (gaps) or rocking of the saddle. The angles of the saddle should match that of your horse, having complete, even contact.

Your western saddle pad should be between one to two inches longer around the saddle to protect the horse's back. The saddle pad should be 1/2 inch to one inch thick and no more to be able to cinch the horse correctly.[6]

Fitting a Breastplate on the Western Saddle:

The breastplate must fit correctly to prevent the saddle from slipping backward and side to side. It attaches to both sides of your saddle skirt's D-rings, either to the cinch or the smaller breastplate D-rings.

A single-strap breastplate should sit just above the point of the shoulder of the horse, giving him enough room to lower and stretch his neck. Y-shaped breastplates sit just above the center point of the horse's chest. Once the breastplate is fastened there should be enough room to fit a fist throughout the breastplate.[7]

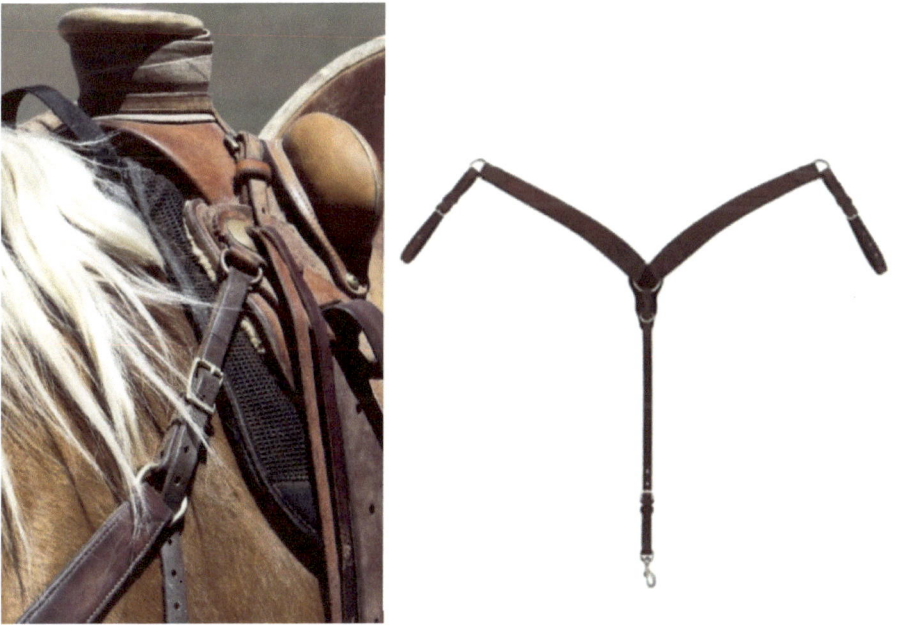

Measuring the Rider for Saddle Fit

English Saddle Rider Fitting Chart:

To measure for a properly fitting saddle, sit with your buttocks at the back of a chair. Then measure from the back of your buttocks to the point of your knee to determine your recommended seat size.

UPPER LEG LENGTH——RECOMMENDED SEAT SIZE

- 0" to 16.5" (41cm).............................15"
- 16.5" to 18.5" (46cm)............................16"
- 18.5 to 20" (50cm)(50cm)...............16.5"
- 20" to 21.5" (54cm)..............................17"
- 21.5" to 23" (58cm)...................................17.5"
- Over 23" (59cm or longer)...........................18"
- Seat size may vary depending on the person's build.

Western Saddle Rider Fitting Chart:

- **Youth:** 12 to 13 inches
- **Small Adult:** 14 inches
- **Large Adult:** 16 inches
- **Extra Large Adult:** 17 inches

There should be approximately 4 inches of space between the front of the rider's body and the fork (swells), and your buttocks should rest against the back of the cantle without pressing on it.

Parts of a Western Saddle

- Horn
- Swell
- Latigo keeper
- Front rigging D-ring
- Latigo
- Deepest part of the seat
- Cantle Point
- Rear rigging D-ring
- Billet Strap
- Stirrup

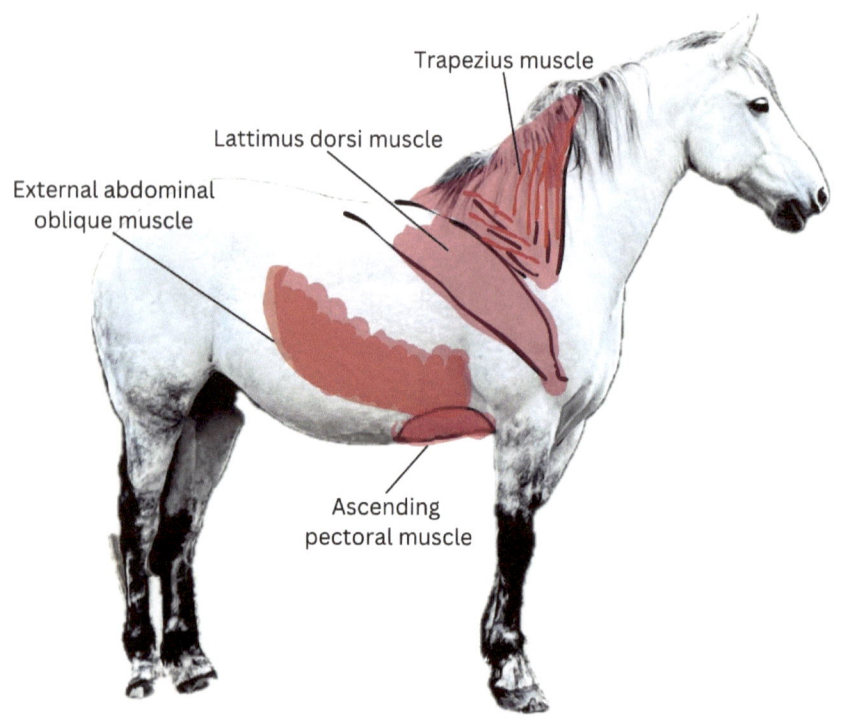

Anatomical structures affected by the girth

English & Western Girth Fitment
How-To-Guide

First and most importantly, the horses's anatomical structures involved with the girth include the *Sternum, Thorax, Ribs 5-7,* and muscle groups of the *Thoracic Sling, Thoracic Ventral Serrated Muscle, Lattissimus Doris Muscle, Ascending Pectoral Muscle,* and the *External Abdominal Oblique.*

It is crucial to have a correctly fitted girth to ensure optimal function of the horse's muscles and nerves. This involves distributing pressure evenly along the attachment points, allowing the horse to breathe and move freely. The peak pressure point of the girth is behind the elbows. Girth tension is lower at a walk than when standing and increases during the trot and canter.

> The horse's ribcage will expand approximately half an inch while riding, and an overly tight girth can negatively impact the horse's performance.[1]

THE GIRTH

The English Girth:
Elastic ends on both sides of the English girth, where they attach to the billets, provide stretch and accomadate the horse's ribcage expansion and contraction. However, they can also contribute to saddle instability. Roller buckles are preferable as they are easier to tighten and do not weaken your leather straps.[2]

English and Western Girth Material:
The girth should be made from breathable and flexible materials to allow the horse's ribcage to expand and contract properly, enabling comfortable breathing and effective sweating. Opt for high-quality leather, string mohair, or wool as these materials offer breathability, stretch, durability, and flexibility, ensuring long-lasting performance.

Western mohair cinch

English mohair girth with rollers

How-To Measure For Girth Size

How-To Measure For The English Girth:

1. Place your saddle pad and saddle on the horse.

2. Run your hand along the horse's barrel, behind the elbow. This is typically where most girths will sit, depending on the horse's confirmation. It's the area of least pressure.

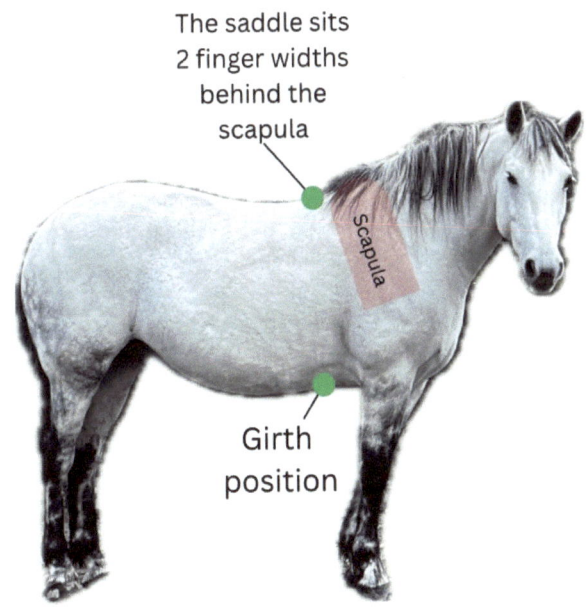

To accurately measure the correct girth size for your horse, follow these steps with the assistance of a fabric measuring tape:

1. Position your saddle on the horse with the saddle pad in place.

2. Locate the middle billet strap on the saddle. These are the three straps underneath the top flap on each side of the saddle.

3. Hold the fabric measuring tape to the middle billet strap at the middle hole.

4. Ensure the measuring tape sits above the horse's elbow so that the elbow will not come into contact with the girth buckles when fastened.

5. Pass the measuring tape under the barrel of the horse to your assistant on the other side.

6. Have your assistant measure to the middle billet strap to the middle hole.

This will ensure you get an accurate measurement for selecting the right girth size, considering the horse's anatomy and comfort.

ENGLISH & WESTERN GIRTH FITMENT

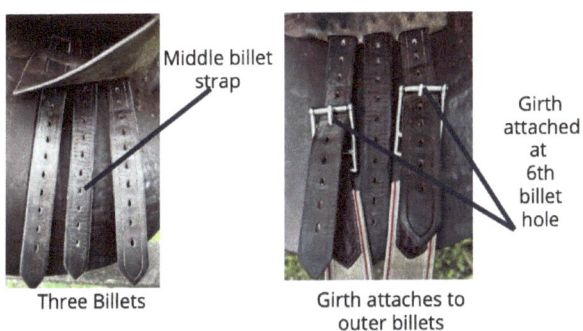

Three Billets — Middle billet strap

Girth attaches to outer billets — Girth attached at 6th billet hole

When buckling the girth, remember it should be buckled to the two outer billets at the middle hole on each side. For example, If there are 12 holes in a billet, place the buckle at the sixth hole, which is the center of the billet holes. This helps keep the saddle centered and prevents the saddle from slipping to one side.

This measurement determines the size of your girth. Girths typically come in two-inch increments. If your measurement falls between two sizes, round up to the next size.

Ensure there is at least two to three finger widths between the saddle pad and the girth. Ideally, use a short girth that is as long as possible to maximize stability when girthed. Position the girth's buckles above the horse's elbow to avoid contact.

Once you've determined your correct girth size, place your saddle and saddle pad on the horse. Attach the girth on the right side of the saddle at the middle holes of the *first and third billets*, and then repeat on the left side. The girth should sit comfortably in the girth area with the least pressure, and you should be able to fit two or three fingers between the horse and the girth to ensure it is not too tight.

When buckling the girth, do so gradually by going up a hole or two on one side and then the other until the saddle is securely in place. After securing the saddle, walk your horse, and recheck the girth.

Ensure the buckles of the girth are positioned above the horse's elbow. The saddle should be snug but not uncomfortably tight, allowing you to snugly slide your fingers along under the sides of the girth for proper fit and adjustment.³

How-To Measure For The Western Cinch:

1. **Locate the measurement point:** Using a measuring tape, find the center of your horse behind the front legs under the belly, where the cinch will sit.

2. **Measure the Ribcage:** Bring the measuring tape up to just below the widest part of the ribcage, which is typically about 4 inches above and behind the elbow.

3. **Calculate the Cinch Size:** Multiply this measurement by two. The result will be your cinch size.

4. **Choosing the Right Size:** Western cinches are available in two-inch increments. If your measurement falls between two sizes, it's recommended to choose the larger size for a better fit and comfort.

Fastening The Western Cinch:

1. **Prepare the Saddle:** Place the saddle pad and saddle on the horse.

2. **Attach the Cinch:** Stand on the left side of the horse. Lift the cinch from underneath the horse and slide the latigo strap through the cinch ring. Pass it down through the D-ring attached to the front of the saddle. Repeat this step twice.

3. **Tighten the Cinch:** Using both hands, lift up on the outside of the latigo strap and pull down on the inside to tighten the cinch.

4. **Secure the Latigo Strap:** Once tightened, slide the end of the latigo strap through the latigo keeper to secure it.[4]

SIGNS YOUR GIRTH MAY NOT FIT

There are several indicators that your girth may not fit properly.

Eight Signs your girth may not fit:

1. Sores or rub marks in the girth area.

2. Swelling, fluid buildup, or girth galls in the girth area.

3. Needing to use the top holes of the girth when tightening.

4. The horse attempts to bite you while girthing.

5. The horse pins its ears back when girthing.

6. The horse swishes its tail during girthing.

7. The horse appears uncomfortable while riding.

8. The horse shows reluctance to move forward or may buck after being girthed.

Finding the Right Fit:
If your horse shows signs that the girth does not fit properly, consider trying a different type or style of girth. There are various options available on the market to ensure you find the perfect fit for your horse's comfort and performance.

PART IV
The Horse's Coat

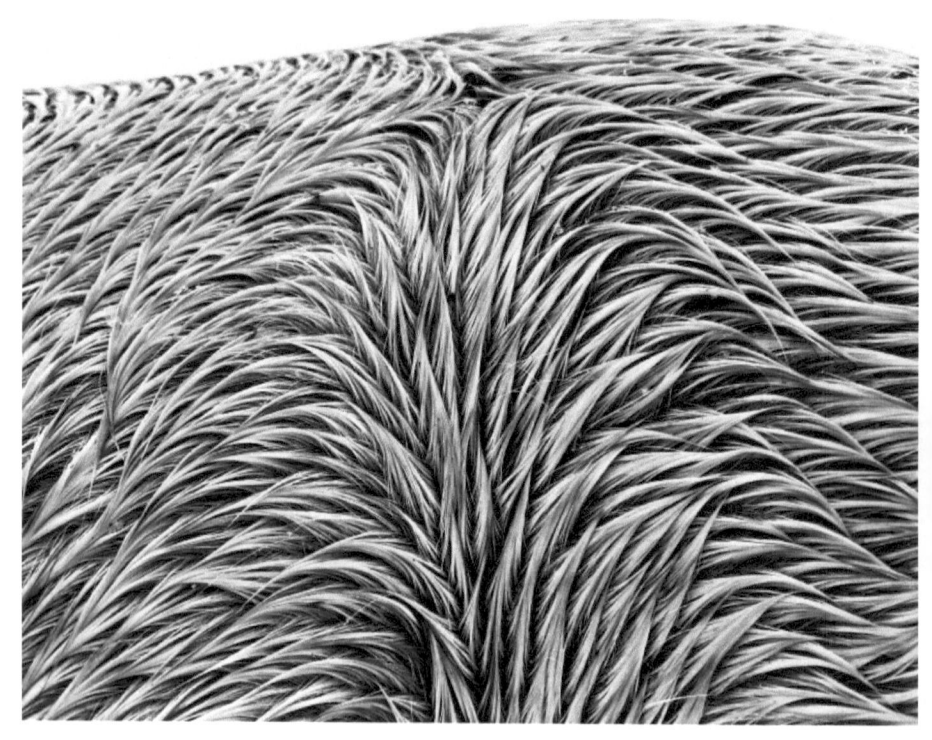

The horse's coat

13

The Horse's Coat

Heat and Humidity, Scratches, Rain Rot, Cooling, Hydration, Hay Consumption, and Blanketing

The horse's coat acts as a protective barrier for its skin, the body's largest organ, shielding the horse from various enviornmental elements like UV rays, wind, rain, and cold. In warmer months, it also helps repel insects. During colder seasons, the coat's hairs stand on end, trapping air to provide insulation and retain body heat, offering an additional layer of warmth[1]

The condition of a horse's coat is a reliable indicator of its overall health and well-being. A shiny, lustrous coat that gleams in the sunlight is typically associated with a healthy horse that receives balanced nutrition. Conversely, a dull, rough, or lifeless coat may indicate an unhealthy horse lacking proper nutrition. The length of a horse's hair can vary based on genetics, breed characteristics, and age.[2]

Heat and Humidity

We all enjoy riding our horses during the summer months, but there are days when it is simply becomes too hot and humid for our horses to be ridden.

Avoid Riding Your Horse:

When the combined air *temperature* plus *humidity* are over 150. For example, if it is 80 degrees Fahrenheit outside and there is 50% humidity, add the 80 degrees to the 50% humidity. 80 + 50 = 130.

Temperature + Humidity	
130 or less	Most effective cooling efficiency.
130-150	Your horse's cooling efficiency is decreased by more than 50% and your horse will be sweating. Take breaks, and cool down throughout training/riding.
150-180	Your horse's ability to regulate its temperature is greatly reduced. May cause heat stress.
180 or more	Your horse is not able to regulate his temperature. Can be fatal.

SWEAT

Sweating is how horses naturally cool themselves, but when humidity is high, less sweat evaporates effectively. In hot weather, a working horse can lose 2-4 gallons of sweat per hour. It's crucial to ensure they have constant access to water.

> On hot days, a horse may drink anywhere from 12-18 gallons of water to stay properly hydrated.

SIGNS OF HEAT EXHAUSTION

- Rapid Breathing (more than 40 breaths per minute).
- Panting.
- Increased Heart Rate.
- Goes from sweating to not sweating.
- Mucous Membranes in the mouth become dry and no longer feel wet or look shiny.
- Rectal Temperature of 104-degrees or more.
- Lethargic.
- Stumbling.

SIGNS OF HEAT STROKE

- The temperature of the horse is 105 and above.

- The horse is dehydrated. Press on the gums of the mouth, they should be pink to white when pressing, and back to pink after a few seconds.

- Dark gums.

- Breathing hard.

- Severe exhaustion.

- Ears flat with head down and very weak.

- Disoriented.

HOW-TO COOL THE HORSE DOWN

- Reduce your ride time and intensity.
- Give electrolytes and free access to salt.
- Cool the horse with a hose by spraying the horse's head, neck, ribs, legs, and back.
- DO NOT hose off the hind end where the bigger muscles are.
- Spray the horse with a steady stream of water until your horse has cooled down.
- DO NOT scrape the horse off after bathing, scraping causes the horse's core temperature to rise again.
- Leg wraps or boots should not be worn, they can cause tendon damage. Bare legs stay cooler.[3]

*Ice baths are safe to cool core temperature, applying to the head, back, neck, and ribs, but **not** the hind end.[4]

WET WEATHER: RAIN ROT AND SCRATCHES

When it rains, horses standing in or walking in wet or muddy areas can experience coat and skin health-related issues. Horses often roll in the mud to repel biting insects, which combined with rain, can compromise their skin and lead to infections like **Rain Rot.** Rain Rot is a contagious form of bacterium living on the horse's skin that becomes active during wet conditions, causing inflammation, lesions, and scabs containing clusters of the horse's hair.

Similarly, horse's can develop an infection known as **Scratches,** concentrated on their lower legs, from prolonged exposure to muddy environments. *Scratches* can be challenging to treat during the wet season.

To prevent theses conditions, keep your horse's coat clean and dry. Regularly wash their body and legs with an anti-microbial shampoo and ensure thorough drying to relieve skin inflammation. Using an anti-microbial spray daily can also help prevent infections. Consult your veterinarian promptly if signs of infection persist, as severe cases of *Scratches* can lead to lameness. Immediate treatment is imperative.[5]

THE HORSE'S COAT

Rain Rot is *contagious* among horses and humans, spreading through contact and shared equipment like brushes, buckets, blankets, and tack. To prevent its spread, clean these items with an anti-microbial soap or shampoo.

Scratches are not contagious and are promoted by a wet environment.

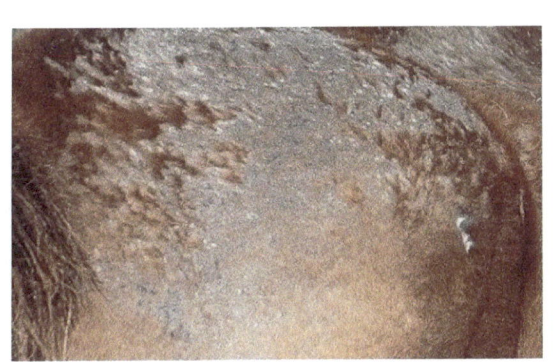

Rain Rot on the horse's body (Contagious)

Scratches (not contagious)

THE HORSE'S WINTER COAT

The horse's winter coat begins to grow in response to daylight shortening, typically starting around mid-August. The natural process prepares the horse for colder weather by increasing hair length.

A natural hair coat is the horse's best defense against cold weather.

A thick winter coat effectively traps warm air next to the horse's skin, providing insulation against cold temperatures. While most horses can withstand cold conditions outdoors, those that are clipped, geriatric, immune-compromised or hard keepers may benefit from blankets. A wet coat will lose insulation. Ensure outdoor horses have access to shelter to shield them from wind, rain, or wet snow.

To help horses generate body heat and stay warm, increase their hay intake during colder weather. Forage is essential as it produces heat through digestion, unlike grain.

Forage equals heat for the horse, not grain.

THE HORSE'S LOWER CRITICAL TEMPERATURE

The lower critical temperature for a horse with a heavy winter coat, on a calm, dry winter day, is around 30 degrees Fahrenheit. As temperatures drop below this critical point, horses require additional hay to maintain body warmth:

- Increase hay by 2 pounds per day for every 10-degree decrease below the 30 degrees Fahrenheit.

- On windy days 10-15 mph at 32 degrees Fahrenheit, add 4-8 pounds of hay.

- In wet, snowy conditions at 32 degrees Fahrenheit without shelter, Add 10-14 pounds more of hay.

> *An average 1000-pound horse typically consumes 15-20 pounds of hay daily in ideal weather conditions.

In extremely cold conditions, horses may struggle to consume enough hay to maintain their weight. Supplementing with good fats like coconut oil, hemp oil, or rice bran can help meet their energy demands. Additionally, consider using a heavyweight blanket with a neck cover to conserve their energy.[6]

Free-choice hay with 24/7 access all winter. Placed throughout the pasture for movement.

HAY CHART

The Average 1000-pound horse consumes approximately 15-20 pounds of hay per day.

Avg. Temperature	Weather	Additional Hay
32° F	10-15 mph wind	4-8 lbs
32° F	Rain	6 lbs
32° F	Rain & Wind	10-14 lbs

Increase the horse's calorie intake heading into winter to maintain good body condition.

Horses who can not escape the elements should have a waterproof blanket with a neck cover. Older horses who can't maintain their body heat, horses with immunity issues, and hard keepers may need blanketing to maintain good body condition.

A very wet snow day called for blanketing

BLANKETING CHART[7]

Blanket as needed.

Blanket	Insulation Grams	Outside Temp.
Sheet	0	50°-65° F
Lightweight	80-180	30°-50° F
Mediumweight	200-300	30°-45° F
Heavyweight	380-440	15°-30° F
Extra Heavyweight	500	Subzero-15°F

Horses exposed to rain or wet snow will lose their natural coat insulation and may need blanketing. Before blanketing, dry the horse's coat, then apply the blanket.

Caring for the Horse in Winter

- Ensure horses have access to water between 45 degrees Fahrenheit and 65 degrees Fahrenheit.
- Feed additional hay as needed to maintain body condition.
- Provide access to a dry shelter with 6 inches of bedding allowing ample space for lying down and stretching out to get REM sleep.
- Monitor the horse's body condition daily.
- Provide 1-2 oz of loose salt daily to encourage drinking.
- Feed a vitamin/mineral supplement as needed for an all forage diet.
- Add good fats like coconut oil, hemp oil, or rice bran for additional calories.
- Provide a blanket with neck coverage for horses without a shelter, hard keepers, and geriatric, or immune-compromised horses.
- Provide blankets with neck coverage for horses out in wet conditions, such as rain and snow.

WATER CONSUMPTION

Horses require increased water intake during winter to prevent dehydration. An average 1000-pound horse may consume 6-12 gallons of water per day or more.

Adequate water intake helps maintain proper fecal moisture levels, preventing dry feces that can lead to colic (abdominal pain), and may lead to death.

> Horses who do not consume enough water will eat less forage throughout the day, and may not have enough energy to tolerate the cold.

Research has found having the horse's drinking water temperature between 45 degrees Fahrenheit and 65 degrees Fahrenheit encourages them to drink more.

Increase the horse's loose salt intake to 1-2 oz a day to trigger a thirst response, and be sure to clean your water buckets daily, to provide them with clean drinking water.[8]

Ensure horses have continuous access to fresh, clean water sources, such as a free-flowing streams in pastures, automatic waterers, or daily bucket cleaning with refills.

24/7 access to water is essential.

NOTES

NOTES

About the Author

Laura A Fitch is a renowned expert in the field of equine bodywork, with a specialization in the Masterson Method®. Laura has made significant contributions to the equine community through extensive travels, where she has shared her expertise by teaching at various clinics and events and running her private equine bodywork business. Laura's deep commitment to equine well-being is further evidenced by her role as the owner and administrator of the popular Facebook page, Students of The Masterson Method®.

Laura possesses a rich and diverse educational background, holding certifications in multiple disciplines. This includes The Masterson Method®, Equinology® Equine Bodywork, Equi-Tape®, Cerebral Spinal Fluid Technique®, and Tucker BioKinetic Module 1. Her pursuit of holistic wellness extends beyond equine practices, as demonstrated by a 200-hour CYT in Vinyasa Yoga. She has also completed Ohio State University's Liberated Hoof Care Course, highlighting a dedication to the comprehensive care of horses.

Laura currently lives in the mountains of North Eastern Pennsylvania with her family and two horses, Loverboy who is featured on the front and back cover, and Dixie, both pictured throughout her book, "The Essential Horse Book: The Complete Guide."

Endnotes

The Key to Equine Well-Being

1. Wendy Williams, The Secret Lives of Horse, long-term observations of wild equines reveal a host of unexpected behaviors, https://www.scientificamerica.com/articles/the-secret-lives-of-horses/

2. Morris Animal Foundation, Equine Feeding Methods: study examines effects on health, well-being, https://phys.org/news/2023-10-equine-methods-effects-health-well-being amp

3. Bachmann, L. Audig'e, M. Stauffarcher, Risk factors associated with behavioral disorders of rib-biting, weaving and box-walking in Swiss horses. Equine Vet J. 2023 Mar;(2): 158-163 PMD: 12638792 DOI: 10.2746/042516403776114216

4. A.A. Logan, B.D. Nelson, R.S. Sehi, E. Jones, C. T. Robinson, A. P. Pease, Short-term stall housing of horses results in changes of bone metabolism, Comparative Excercise Physiology: 15(4)-Pages 283-290, https://doi.org/10.3920CEP190038 August 27, 2019

5. Patricia M. Graham-Thiers PhD, L. Kristen Bowen BA, Improved Ability to Maintain Fitness in Horses During Large Pasture Turnout, https://doi.org/10.106/j.jevs.2012.09.001

6. Jessica Carvalho Seabra, Marcos Martinez do Vale, Katarine Maria Spercoski, Tanja Hess, Penelope Patricia Viviani de Moura, Joao Ricardo Dittrich, Journal of Equine Veterinary Science, volume 13, December 2023. Time-Budget and Welfare Indications of Stabled Horses in Three Different Stall Architectures: A Cross-Sectional Study, https://doi.org/10.1016.j.jevs

7. Michigan State University, MSU Extension, Behavioral Considerations When Housing Horses, April 12, 2012, Christine Shelly, https://www.canr.msu.edu/resource/behavioral-considerations-when-housing-horses

8. Colorado State University, Extension, Paddock Paradise Track System for Horses, by Jennifer Cook, *Small Acreage Management Coordinator, NRCS/CSU Extension,* https://sam.extension.colostate.edu/topics/pasture-range/paddock-paradise-track-system-for-horses/

9. https://digitalcommons.wku,edu/cgi/viewcontent.cgi?article=1069&context=theses

10. J Anim Physiol Anim Nutr (Berl). 2022 Marc, 106(2): 313-326. Published online 2021 Sept 22. doi: 10.111/pn.13643

11. University of Kentucky, Department of Animal & Food Sciences, *Martin-Gutton College of Agriculture, Food and Enviornment,* Colic in Horses Fernannda C. Camargo, Animal and Food Sciences, https://afs,ca.uky.edu

12. University of Minnesota Extension, Colic in your horse, Erin Malone, DVM, https://extension.umn.edu/horse-health/colic-your-horse#:~:text=Signs%20of%20colic%252

13. Oregon State University, OSU Extension Service, A Horse's Guide to Pasture-Associated Laminitis, Scott Duggan and Troy Downing, https://extension.oregonstate.edu/catalog/pub/em-9354-horse-owners-guide-pasture-associated-laminitis

14. PennVet New Bolton Center University of Pennsylvania, Van Eps Laminitis and Endocrinology Laboratory, https://vet.upenn.edu/research

15. UC Davis Veterinary Medicine, Center for Equine Health Laminitis, Amy Young, March 23, 2020, https://ceh.vetmed.ucdavis.edu/health-topics/laminitis

16. Western Kentucky University, Morgan Nicole Akers, Effects of Early Spring Growth Annual Ryegrass Pasture Consumption on Parameters Associated with Laminitis in Horses,(2009). *Masters Theses & Specialist Projects.* Paper 71. https://digitalcommons.wku.edu/theses/71

17. University of Minnesota Extension, Krishoa Martinson, Extension Equine Specialist, https://extension.umn.edu/horse-nutrition/grazing-horses-prone-laminitis

A Healthy Horse

1. Minnesota Horse Welfare Coalition, Keeping horses safe at home, https://www.minnesotahorsewelfare.org/henneke-body-condition-scoring#

2. Assessing the Health and Well-being of Horses, Jan 21, 2020, Health, Horses, Colleen Brady, Ed Pajar, Janice Sojka, Nicole Buck, John Bern's, Mark Russell, Department of Animal Sciences, Purdue University Department of Veterinary Clinical Sciences, Purdue University and Department of Animal Sciences, Michigan State University, https://horses.extension.org/assesing-the-health-and-well-being-of-horses/

3. Penn State Extension, How to Take Your Horse's Vital Signs, https://extension.psu.edu/how-to-take-your-horses-vital-signs

4. Penn State Extension, Recognizing a Healthy Horse, June 12, 2023, https://extension.psu.edu/recognizing-a-healthy-horse

The Equine Mind

1. Murphy, J., Arkins, S (2007). Equine learning behavior. Behavioral Processes, 76(1), 1-13.

2. Hanggi, E.B (2005). The Thinking Horse: Cognition and perception reviewed. Proceedings of the American Association of Equine Practitioners, 51, 246-255.

3. Krueger, K. & Flauger, B. (2011). Social learning in horses from a novel perspective. Animal Cognition, 14(3), 451-462.

4. Proops, L., McComb, K., & Reby, D. (2013). Cross-modal individual recognition in domestic horses (Equus caballus). Proceedings of the National Academy of Sciences, 106(3), 947-951.

5. McGreevy, P., & McLean, A. (2010). Equitation Science. Wiley-Blackwell.

6. Christenson, J.W., Rundgren, M., & Olsson, K. (2006). Training methods for horses: Habituation to a frightening stimulus. Applied Animal Behavior Science, 101(1-2), 1-11.

7. McBride, S. D., & Cuddeford, D. (2001). The putative welfare-reducing effects of preventing equine stereotypic behaviour. Animal Welfare, 10(2), 173-189.

8. Skinner, B.F. (1938). The Behavior of Organisms: An experimental Analysis. Appleton-Century.

9. McGreevy, P., & McLean, A. (2010). Equitation Science. Wiley-Blackwell.

10. Sankey, C., Richard-Yris, M. A., Leroy, H., Henry, S., & Hausberger, M. (2010). Positive interactions lead to lasting positive memories in horses, Equus caballus. Animal Behavior, 79(4), 869-875.

11. Konstanze, Kruger, Equine Behaviour Team, Ecology of Social Learning and Cognition in Horses, Research, Forschung, Equine, Pferd, Horse, Equine-behavior.de

12. Cathrynne Henshall, Hayley Randle, Nidhish Francis, and Rafael Freire, *Scientific Reports*, The effects of stress and exercise on the learning performance of horses, nature.com

13. Kiyohito Iigaya, Madalena S. Fonseca, Masayoshi Murakami, Zachary F. Mainen & Peter Dayan, Nature Communications 9, Article number:24777 (2018). An effect of serotonergic stimulation on learning rates For rewards apparent after long intertrials intervals

14. Nicol, C. J. (2002). Equine learning: Progress and suggestions for future research. Applied Animal Behaviour Science, 78(2-4), 193-208. Retrieved from Elsevier.

15. Hanggi, E.B. (1999). Categorizing learning in horse (Equus caballus). Journal of Comparative Psychology. 113(3), 243-252. Retrieved from APAPsycNet.

16. Murphy, J., & Arkins, S. (2007). Equine learning behaviour. Behavioural Processes, 76(1), 1-13.

17. McGreevy, P., & McLean, A. (2010). Equitation Science. Wiley-Blackwell. Available at Wiley.

18. Proops, L., McComb, K., & Reby, D (2013). Cross-modal individual recognition in domestic horses (Equus caballus). Proceedings of the National Academy of Sciences, 106(3), 947-951.

19. Maier S.; Seligmman M; Learned Helplessness: Theory and evidence. Journal of Experimental Psychology; Volume 105, March 1976-3-46

20. Long-term memory formation in equine hippocampal structures, Journal of Veterinary Psychology, Vol. 14, pp. 60-67.

21. Equine memory and hippocampal function, Neurobiology of Animals, Vol. 22, pp. 312-318.

22. "Photographic memory in equines: Detail recall and sensory association", Animal Memory Review, Vol. 8, pp. 102-108

Vision, Hearing, Smell

1. Iowa State University Extension and Outreach, Equine Science. Vision in the Equine, Blog, Vision, https://www.extension.iastate.edu/equine/vision-equine

2. Megan Elizabeth Morgan, Temple Grandin, Sarah Kristen Matlock, Evaluating the Reaction to a Complex Rotated Object in the American Quarter Horse (Equus caballus), May 2021 Animals 11(5):1383, 11(5):1383, DOI:10.3390/ani11051383, License CC BY 4.0

3. Troy Griffith, Horse Vision And Its Effects on Horsemanship, Horse Network, https://horsenetwork.com/2016/07/horse-vision-effects-horsemanship/

4. Ashley Griffin, University of Kentucky, Horse Hearing, July 31, 2019/Horses-Training and Behavior, https://horses.extension.org/horse-hearing/

5. Kentucky Research Staff, Oct 1, 2018, Handlers Voice Impacts Human Horse Bond, https://ker.com/equinenews/handlers-voice-impacts-human/-horse-bond

6. Medical News today, Takimoto, Ayaka, https://medicalnewstoday.com/articles/322234#How-Horses-Respond-to-human-faces,-voices

7. Vilain Rorvang, Maria Neilsen, L. Birte and Andrew Neil Mclean/ Sensory Abilities of Horses and Their Importance for Equitation Science 2020 Sep.9,doi:10.3389/fvets.2020.00633, https://www.ncbinim.nih.gov/pmc/articles/

8. Beaver, B. (2020). *Equine Behavioral Medicine*. Academic Press.

9. Roving, M. V., Nielsen, B. L., & Mclean, A. N. (2020). *Sensory Abilities of Horses and their Importance for Equitation Science.* Front. Vet. Sci, 7:633.

Anatomy of The Horses's Teeth

1. Mojave River Equine Veterinary Service, Learning Center, How to properly care for your equine animal, https://mojaveRivereq uine.com/Learn/

2. American Association of Equine Practitioners, Guide For Determining The Age Of The Horse, Aging Horses by Teeth-AAEP.pdf

3. Wayne Loch, Melvin Bradley, Department of Animal Sciences, University of Missouri Extension, Determining Age of Horses by their Teeth, May 1998

4. Revised by Carl Hooper, DVM, Utah State University Equine Extention Specialist, Ageing Horses by Their Teeth, Revised May 2020

5. Conley Koontz Equine Hospital, Equine Dentistry, https://ckeq uinehospital.com/page/175/Equine-Dentist.ry

6. KBHH Common Horse Dental Problems, https://www.msd-animal-health-hub.co.uk/Healthy-Horses/Health/DentalProblems/

7. Karl Hoppes, DVM, Utah State University Equine Extension Specialist, Utah State University Equine Extension, Aging Horses by their Teeth, https://www.extension.usu/equine/research/agi ng-horses-by-their-teeth.

8. Jack Easley, DVM,M,DAVDC (Equine), DABVP (EQ) Easley Equine Dentistry, Shelbyville, KY, Dental Disorders of Horses, Chicago. "The Merck Manual," white house station, NJ Merck & Co., INC.n.d. https://www.merckvetmanual.com/horse-owners/digestive-disorders-ofhore/dental-disorders-of-horses

The Digestive System

1. Digestive Anatomy and Physiology of the Horse blog Equine Extension, Equine Nutrition Iowa State University Extension and Outreach, Equine Science, https://www.extension.iastate.edu/equine/search/content/digestion

2. Miriam Baumgartner, Theresa Boisson, Michael H. Erhard, and Margit H Zeitler-Feicht, Common Feeding Practices Pose A Risk to the Welfare of the Horse When Kept on Non-Edible Bedding, https://ncbi,nim,nih.gov/pmc/articles/PMC7142811/

3. Dr. Samantha Wellspring, Winter Feeding Guidelines from Dr. Samantha Wellsping, https://wildfedhorse.com/blogs/wild-fed-journal/winter-feeding-guidelines-fro

4. Elizabeth Share, MS, 4-H Livestock Program Specialist, The Ohio State University Sara L. Mastellar, Ph.D. Equine Faculty, Ohio State University Agricultural Technical Institute, Haley M. Zynda, NS, Extension Educator, Wayne County, The Gastrointestinal Tract of The Horse, Ohio State University, College of Food, Agricultural and Environmental Sciences, https://ohioonline.osu.edu./fact sheet/1022

5. Colette Ermers, Nerida McGilchrist, Kate Fenner, Bethany Wilson, Paul McGreevy, The Fibre Requirements of Horses and the Consequences and Causes of Failure to meet them, https://pubmed.ncbi.nim.nih.gov/37106977

6. Amy Young, July 29, 2019 Equine Gastric Ulcer Syndrome, What are gastric ulcers? https://ceh.vetmed.ucdavis.edu/health-topics/equine-gastric-ulcer-syndrome#

The Equine Hoof

1. U. Yxklinten1 and Y. Sharp2, theequinedocumentalist, Nov 10, 2023, The quantification and definition of a new hoof balance paradigm. https://www.theequinedocumentalist.com/post/the-quantification-and-definition-of-a-new-hoof-balance-paradigm

2. LeMaster C, LeMaster CW. Equine Hoof Care. Clemson (SC): Clemson Cooperative Extension, Land-Grant Press by Clemson Extension; 2022 Jun.LGP 1136. Https://lgpress.clemson.edu/publication/equine-hoof-care/

3. The University of Nottingham, July 27, 2019, Royal Society Interface Journal, Physics of animal health: On the machanobiology of hoof growth and form. http://doi.org/10.1098/rsif.2019.0214

4. Robert C. McClure, Department of Veterinary Anatomy, College of Veterinary Medicine, Functional Anatomy of the Horse Foot, https://extension.missouri.edu/publication/g2740

5. Jayne Hunt (www.healthyhooves.co.uk), The Equine Podiatry Association, Hoof Anatomy- A Beginners Guide, https://www.epauk.org/about-equine-podiatry/articles/hoof-anatomy-a-beginners-guide.

6. Mattia A. Gunkelman, Carolyn J. Hanner, Department of Animal Science, North Dakota State University, Fargo, ND, A preliminary Study Examining the Digital Cushion in Horses, Journal of Equine Veterinary Science, https://www.sciencedirect.com/science/abs/pii/S0737080616303756

7. Duggan J. Scott, Livestock Extension Faculty, Horse Hoof and Leg Anatomy: A Guide Tour, https.//extention.oregonstate.edu/sites/default/files/documents/912/osu-version-horse-hoof-leg-anatomy.pdfextentionoregonstate.edu

8. Haemodynamic Mechanism-The Key to Hoof Health, the equine documentarist, https://www.theequinedocumentalist.com/post/haedynamic-mechanism-the-key-to-hoof-health

9. O'GradySE: Strategies for shoeing the horse with palmer foot pain. *Proceedings of the 52nd annual Convention of the American Association of Equine Practitioners.* 2006

10. Robert J. Hunt DVM, MS, Farriery for the Hoof with Low or Underrun Heels, 12 September 2012, https://doi.org/10.1016/j.cveq.2012.06.002

11. Pete Ramey, Heel Height: The Deciding Factor 10-13-05, https://www.hoofrehab.com/HeelHeight.html

A Guide To Parasite Prevention

1. Martin Nielsen, DVM, PhD, Dipl.ACVM, associate professor of parasitology at the University of Kentucky's Maxwell H. Gluck Equine Research Center, Why Equine Fecal Egg Count Matters, https://horseman'slab.com/worm-info.html

2. J.C. Gould, M.G. Rossano, L.M. Lawrence, S.V. Burn, R.B. Ennis, E.T. Lyons "The effects of windrow composting on the viability of parascaris quorum eggs." Veterinary Parasitology, Volume 191 Issues. 1-2 January 2013 pages 73-80, https://www.sciencedirect.com/article/abs/pii/s030440171200430x

3. Jennie A H Crawley, Simon N. Chapman, Virpi Lummaa, Carly L. Lynsdale, Testing storage methods of faecal samples for subsequent measurement of helminth egg numbers in the domestic horse, vet para 2016 May 15; 221:130-3 dot:10.1016/j.vetpar.2016.03.012 Pub 2016 Mar 16., https://pubmed.ncbi.nim.nih.gov/27084484

4. Laurent Herbert, Julian Cauchard, Pauline Dogleg, Lola Quitard, Claire Laurie, Sandrine Petry, Viability of Rhodocoddus equi and parascaris quorum eggs exposed to high temperatures. Curt Microbio. 2010 Jan;60 (1) : 38-41.doi:10.1007/s00284-009-9497-5. Pub 2009 Sep 1., https://pubmed.ncbi.nim.nih.gov/1972741

5. MSD 2023 Merck & Co, Inc. Types of Parasites and Worms in Horses. https://msd-animal-health-hub.co.uk/Healthy-Horses/Health/Parasites-Worms

6. Westgate Labs, Top 10 Ways to Slow Resistance https://www.westgatelabs.co.uk/info-zone/resistance-to-wormers/top-10-ways-to-slow-resistance/

7. Horsemen's laboratory, https://horsemmenslab.com/faq.html

The Best Sleep Practices

1. Linda Greening and Sabastian McBride, A Review of Sleep: Implications for Equine Welfare, front vet sci. 2022:9-916737, 2022 Aug 17. Dot:10.3389/fvets.2022.916737, National Library of Medicine, https://ncib.nim.nih.gov/PMC/articles/PMC9428463/

2. Monica Aleman, MVZ, PhD, Diplomate ACIM; Colette D Williams, BS; and Terrell Holiday, DVM, PhD. Diplomate ACIM, Sleep and Sleep Disorders in Horses, https://aaep.org/sites/default/files/proceedings-o8 proceedings-Z9100108000180.pdf

3. Daniela Amiounty, Thesis, December 15, 2020 Bedding and Light Levels Found to Affect Horse's Sleep, https://www.yourhorse.co.UF/horse-care/bedding-and-light-level-found-to-affect-horses-sleep/

4. Linda Greening, Josh Downing, Daniella Amiouny, Line Lekang, Sebastian McBride; The Effect of Altering Routine Husbandry Factors on Sleep Duration and Memory Consolidation in the Horse Equine Department, https://pure.hartpury.ac.uk/en/publications/the-effect-of-altering-Routine-husbandry-factors-on-sleep-duration-3

Bridle and Halter Fitting Guide

1. Vetphysiophyle, Equine Cranial Nerves, https://vetphysiophyle.co.uk/2019/04/04/equine-cranial-nerves/

2. Equine Cranial Nerves-Horse-Anatomy-wikivetenglish, https://en.wikivet.net/Equine_Cranial_Nerves_-_Horse_Anatomy

3. C. A. Haun, Consultant Editor, in The Equine Manual (Second Edition), 2006, The Nervous System, Facial Nerve Paralysis.

4. Paul McGreevy, Amanda Warren-Smith, Yann Guisard, Journal of Veterinary Behavior, Volume 7, Issue 3, May-June 2012, Pages 142-148

5. Neimark MA: (teal) Vibrissa resonance as a transduction mechanism for tactile encoding. 2003, Journal of Neuroscience 23:6499-6509

6. British Horse Society. (2021) Sensory Hairs, https://www.bhs.org.uk/horse-care-and-welfare/health-care-management/horse-health/sensory-hairs/#

7. The Briitish Horse Society, Impacts of whisker trimming on the horse, https://bhs.org.uk/horse-care-and-welfare/health-care-management/horse=health/sensory-hairs/

8. Federation Equestre Internationale (FEI) (2021) 2022 Veterinary Regulations Article 1004 Prohibited Methods 06 Aug 2021 BEVA, https://www.beva.org.uk/News/Latest-News/Details/FEI-Veterinary-Regulations-Article-1004-Prohibited-Methods

9. McGreevy, P(2012) Equine behavior. A guide for Veterinarians and Equine Scientists. Second Edition. Elsevier Health Sciences., P. 49:,(2004)+Equine+behaviour+A+guide+for+veterinarians+and+equine+scientist.+Saunders,+Elservoir+Ltd,

Saddle Fit

1. Kentucky Research Staff, March 28, 2022, Study: Horses Mature Enough For Athlete Endeavors by Two Years Old. Https://ker.com/equinenews/study-horses-mature-enough-for-athletic-endevears-by-two-years-old/

2. Equine Skeletal Development {Charts& Animation} https://www.horsesandus.com/equine-skeletal-developement/

3. Master Saddlers Association, Points of Saddle Fitting/www.mastersaddlers.com/points.htm

4. Robert McCann-Master Saddler Pony Club Victoria, Saddle Fitting, https://www.youtube.com/watch?v=esdpFgugP34

5. Kate Ballard, Society of Master Saddlery, How To Tell if your saddle fits, https://www.youtube.com/watch?v=ht4izu65gD4

6. Rod Nikkel/Mythbusting-"The Exterior Abdominal Vein" https://www.rodnikkel.com/saddle-tree-blog-from-shop-and-desk/mythbusting-the-exteriorAbdominalVein/

7. Equus, March 10, 2017, How to fit your Horse's Breastplate, https:/equusmagazine.com/behavior/Howtofit-your-Horse'ssbreastplate/

English & Western Girth Fitment

1. MSC.Martha Kulikoeska, correct girth fitting- A key issue for overall comfort of the horse, https://www.winderen.com/en/news/154/correct-girth-fitting-a-key-issue-for-overall-comfort-of-the-horse

2. Dr. Russell Mackechnic-Guire, How girths have been scientifically proven to have an impact on performance, March 2 5, 2020, https://trainermagazine.com/european-trainer-articles/how-girths-have-been-scientifically-proven-to-have-an-impact-on-performance/2020/3/24

3. Murray, R.et al, The Veterinary Journal/2013. https://quintic.com/research/Girth%20Pressure.pdf

4. Warwick Schiller, how to tighten cinch, Doing up the girth on a western saddle, https://www.youtube.com/watch?v=On-HHHCuawfi

The Horse's Coat

1. Karen Waite, Michigan State Extension, and MSU Department of Animal Science-October 25, 2012, Equine Winter Hair Coats 101, https:www.Canr.MSU.edu/news/equine_winter_hair_coats_101

2. Christine Barakat, The Long & Short of Equine Coats, The Secret to bringing out your horse's natural shine lies in understanding how his hair grows. June 12, 2022, https://equusmagazine.com/horse-care/long-short-equine-coats-31988/

3. Maryland Horse Council, Riding in Hot Weather, https://mdhorsecouncil.org/riding-in-hot-weather/

4. Krishona Martinson, Extension equine specialist; Marcia Hathaway, professor of animal science, College of Food, Agriculture and Natural Resource Sciences; Chris Ward DVM; Roy Johnson Cargill Animal Nutrition, caring for horses during hot weather, University of Minnesota Extension, https://extension.umn.edu/horse-care-and-management/caring-horses-during-hot-weather#treatment-1301562

5. Brittani Kirkland, former Extension Educator, Equine, Pennsylvania State University, Horse Management During Wet Weather, https://extension-psu.edu/horse-management-during-wet-weather

6. Equine Cold Weather Care, Total Equine Veterinary Associate's TEVApedia, https://totalequinevets.com/client-center/resources/TEVApedia/equine-cold-weather-care

7. Horse Blanketing 101, Learn all about blanketing Your Horse, https://www.sstack.com/Resources/Schneiders-learning-center-blanketing-101/

8. Caring for your horse in the winter, University of Minnesota Extension, https://extension.unn.edu/horse-care-and-management/caring-your-horse-winter#

www.ingramcontent.com/pod-product-compliance
Lightning Source LLC
Chambersburg PA
CBHW040933030426
42337CB00001B/3